REWARD
Intermediate
Teacher's Book

Heinemann English Language Teaching
Halley Court, Jordan Hill, Oxford OX2 8EJ
A division of Reed Educational & Professional Publishing Limited

OXFORD MADRID ATHENS PARIS FLORENCE PRAGUE SÃO PAULO
CHICAGO MELBOURNE AUCKLAND SINGAPORE TOKYO IBADAN
GABORONE JOHANNESBURG PORTSMOUTH (NH)

Heinemann is a registered trademark of
Reed Educational & Professional Publishing Limited

ISBN 0 435 242113 (Teacher's Notes)
ISBN 0 435 240269 (Interleaved)

Text © Simon Greenall, 1995
Design and illustrations © Reed Educational & Professional
Publishing Limited 1995
First published 1995.

Designed by Stafford & Stafford
Cover design by Stafford & Stafford
Cover illustration by Martin Sanders

Illustrations by:
Adrian Barclay (Beehive Illustration), pp3, 22, 23, 26, 37, 73;
Hardlines, pp27, 76;
David Mostyn, pp8/9, 12/13, 46, 96;
Martin Sanders, pp18/19, 24/25, 37, 40/41, 44, 48, 56/57, 58, 63, 64,
66, 67, 68/69, 78, 85, 90, 94;
Simon Stafford, p10.

Commissioned photography by:
Roger Charlesson pp20/21, 30 (Batman), 54/55, 90;
Chris Honeywell pp8/9, 14, 34, 35, 74/75.

Author's Acknowledgements
I am very grateful to all the people who have contributed towards
Reward Intermediate. My thanks are due to:
- All the teachers I have worked with on seminars around the world,
  and the various people who have influenced my work.
- James Richardson for producing the tapes, and the actors for their
  voices.
- The various schools who piloted the material, especially Michelle
  Zahran at Godmer House, Oxford School of English, Oxford; Jon Hird
  at the Lake School, Oxford; Philip Kerr at International House, London.
- The Lake School, Oxford and especially Sue Kay for allowing me to
  observe classes.
- The readers, all of whom wrote encouraging and constructive reports.
- Simon Stafford for his first class design.
- Jacqueline Watson for researching the photos so efficiently.

- Chris Hartley for his continual advice and encouragement.
- Angela Reckitt for taking over as editor so calmly and effectively.
- Catherine Smith for her thorough and considerate management of
  the project.
- and last, but by no means least, Jill, Jack, Alex and Grace.

Acknowledgements
The authors and publishers would like to thank the following for their
kind permission to reproduce material in this book:
Rogers, Coleridge & White Ltd for an extract from *The Tropical
Traveller* © John Hatt, 1982; Reed Consumer Books for an extract
from *It can't be true* and *The world's greatest mysteries* © Octopus
Books; *The Independent on Sunday* for an extract from 'A Pilgrim's
Package' by David Lodge and 'Nothing beats a good rant' by Rosalind
Twist; Anvil Press Poetry for the inclusion of 'Valentine', a poem from
Mean Time by Carol Ann Duffy; *The Observer* for an extract from
'Memories are made of this' by David Randall and 'Breaking the rules'
by Norman Harris; Premier Magazines for an extract from 'All dressed
in red' by Alexandra Davison and 'Wild and beautiful' by Brian
Jackman, first printed in British Airways *High Life* magazine; Hamish
Hamilton Ltd for an extract from *A Year in Provence* by Peter Mayle
© Peter Mayle, 1989; Michael Joseph Ltd for an extract from
Superhints compiled by The Lady Wardington; Mandarin Paperbacks
(an imprint of Reed International Books) for an extract from *The
Good Tourist* by Katie Wood and Syd House; Random House UK Ltd,
for an extract from *Beyond Belief* by Ron Lyon and Jenny Paschall;
Randall Brink for the inclusion of an extract from 'Life Stories: Amelia
Earhart; the unsolved mystery', as published by *Marie Claire*
magazine, June 1994; Lonely Planet Publications for an extract from
Hong Kong – a travel survival kit by Robert Storey (May 1992); *The
Independent* for an extract from 'Christmastime for everyone' by
Terry McCarthy; Rough Guides Ltd for an extract from *Rough Guide
to Australia.*

Photographs by: Aquarius p30; Art Directors pp38/39; The Anthony
Blake Photo Library p62; Micheal Busselle p44(t); Mary Evans Picture
Library p82 (detail); Sarita Sharma/Format p6; Joanie O'Brian/Format
p42; Maggie Murray/Format p43; Chrispin Hughes p28; The Hulton
Deutsch Collection Ltd p82; The Image Bank pp32,86; Images
Colour Library pp42,92; The Kobal Collection p31; National Film
Archive pp50/51; Pictor International p92; Science and Society
Picture Library p16(t); Catherine Smith/Matthew Sherrington pp80,
81; Spanish National Tourist Office p44(b); Simon Stafford p76; Tony
Stone Images pp32/33, 42, 43, 52, 70(a), 70(b), 88, 89; The Telegraph
Colour Library pp70(c), 98; Topham Picture Source p16(b); Eye
Ubiquitous p42; Jacqueline Watson p80(t); Zefa Picture Library p4.

The publishers would also like to thank Becky Jones, Daphne Levens
and Guy Lowe.

While every effort has been made to trace the owners of copyright
material in this book, there have been some cases when the publishers
have been unable to contact the owners. We should be grateful to hear
from anyone who recognises their copyright material and who is
unacknowledged. We shall be pleased to make the necessary amend-
ments in future editions of the book.

97 98 99 10 9 8 7 6 5 4 3 2

Printed and bound in Great Britain by
M & A Thomson Litho Limited, East Kilbride.

Introduction

Course organisation

Reward is a general English course which will take adult and young adult learners of English from elementary level to advanced level. British English is used as the model for grammar, vocabulary, spelling and pronunciation, but other varieties of English are included for listening and reading practice. The course components for each level are as follows:

For the student	For the teacher
Student's Book	Teacher's Book
Practice Book	Class cassettes
Practice Book cassette	Resource Pack
	Business Resource Pack

The Student's Book has forty teaching lessons and eight Progress check lessons. After every five teaching lessons there is a Progress check lesson to review the language covered in the preceding teaching lessons and to present new language work relevant to the grammar, functions and topics covered so far. Within the teaching lessons, the main grammar or language functions and the most useful vocab-ulary are presented in boxes which allow easy access to the principal language of the lesson. This makes the focus of the lesson clearly accessible for purposes of presentation and revision. Each lesson will take about 90 minutes.

The two **Class cassettes** contain all the listening and sounds work in the Student's Book.

The Practice Book has forty practice lessons correspond-ing to the forty teaching lessons in the Student's Book. The Practice Book extends work done in class with the Student's Book by providing further practice in grammar, vocabulary, reading, writing, listening and sounds work. The activities are designed for self-access work and can be used either in the class or as self-study material. Each lesson will take between 45 and 60 minutes. An answer key is included for self-checking.

The **Practice Book cassette** contains all the listening and sounds work in the Practice Book.

The Teacher's Book contains a presentation of the course design, methodological principles, as well as detailed teaching notes interleaved with pages from the Student's Book. It also includes four photocopiable tests. The teach-ing notes for each lesson include a step-by-step guide to teaching the lesson, a discussion of some of the difficulties the learners may encounter, and more detailed methodolo-gical issues arising from the material presented.

The Resource Packs provide additional teaching material to practise the main language points of the teaching lessons. *Reward* is designed to be very flexible in order to meet the very different requirements of learners. There is a Resource Pack for learners of general English and a Business Resource Pack for learners with language requirements of a more professional nature.

Each pack contains a wide variety of communicative prac-tice activities in the form of photocopiable worksheets with step-by-step Teacher's Notes on the back. There is at least one activity for each lesson in the Student's Book and the activities can be used to extend a core teaching lesson of 90 minutes from the Student's Book with an average of 30 minutes of extra material for use in the classroom. They can also be used to revise specific structures, language or vocabulary later in the course.

As well as step-by-step Teacher's Notes for each activity, each Resource Pack includes an introduction which explains how to use the worksheets and offers tips on how to get the most out of the activities.

Course design

The course design is based on a broad and integrated multi-syllabus approach. It is broad in the sense that it covers grammar and language functions, vocabulary, reading, listening, speaking, writing and sounds explicitly, and topics, learner training and socio-cultural competence implicitly. It is integrated in that each strand of the course design forms the overall theme of each lesson. The lessons always include activities focusing on grammar and language functions, and vocabulary. They also include reading, listening, speaking, writing and sounds. The inclusion of each strand of the syllabus is justified by its communicative purpose within the activity sequence. The methodological principles and approaches to each strand of course design are discussed below.

Methodological principles

Here is an outline of the methodological principles for each strand of the course design.

Grammar and language functions

Many teachers and learners feel safe with grammar and language functions. Some learners may claim that they want or need grammar, although at the same time suggest that they don't enjoy it. Some teachers feel that their learners' knowledge of grammar is demonstrable proof of language acquisition. But this is only partly true. Mistakes of grammar are more easily tolerated than mistakes of vocabulary, as far as comprehension is concerned, and may be more accept-able than mistakes of socio-cultural competence, as far as behaviour and effective communication is concerned. *Reward* attempts to establish grammar and language functions in their pivotal position but without neglecting the other strands of the multi-syllabus design.

Vocabulary

There are two important criteria for the inclusion of words in the vocabulary boxes. Firstly, they are words which the intermediate learner should acquire in order to com-municate successfully in a number of social or transactional situations. The revised Threshold Level (1990)[1] has been used to arbitrate on the final selection. Secondly, they may also be words which, although not in Threshold Level, are generated by the reading or listening material and are con-sidered suitable for the intermediate level. However, an overriding principle operates: there is usually an activity which allows learners to focus on and, one hopes, acquire the words which are personally relevant to them. This involves a process of personal selection or grouping of words according to personal categories. It is hard to acquire words which one doesn't need, so this approach responds to the learner's individual requirements and personal moti-vation. Intermediate *Reward* presents approximately 950 words in the vocabulary boxes for the learner's active attention, but each learner must decide which words to focus on. The *Wordbank* in the Practice Book encourages students to store the words they need in categories which are relevant to them.

Reading

The reading passages are generally at a higher level than one might expect for learners at intermediate level. Foreign language users who are not of near-native speaker competence are constantly confronted with difficult language, and to expose the learners to examples of real-life English in the reassuring context of the classroom is to help prepare them for the conditions of real life. There is always an activity or two which encourages the learner to respond to the passage either on a personal level or to focus on its main ideas. *Reward* attempts to avoid a purely peda-gogical approach to reading, and encourages the learner to respond to the reading passage in a personal and genuine way before using it for other purposes.

Listening

Listening is based on a similar approach to reading in *Reward*. Learners are often exposed to examples of natural, authentic English in order to prepare them for real-life situations in which they will have to listen to ungraded English. But the tasks are always graded for the learners' particular level. Learners at intermediate level are often pleased by how much they understand. Learners at higher levels are often disappointed by how little they understand. A number of different native and non-native accents are used in the listening passages to reflect the fact that in real life very few speakers using English speak with standard British or American pronunciation.

Speaking

Many opportunities are given for speaking, particularly in pairwork and groupwork. Learners are encouraged to work in pairs and groups, because the number of learners in most classes does not allow the teacher to give undivided atten-tion to each learner's English. In these circumstances, it is important for the teacher to evaluate whether fluency or accuracy is the most important criterion. On most occasions in Intermediate *Reward* speaking practice in the Grammar sections is concerned with accuracy, and in the Speaking sections with fluency. In the latter sections, it is better not to interrupt and correct the learners until after the activity has finished.

Writing

The writing activities in *Reward* are based on guided paragraph writing with work on making notes, turning notes into sentences, and joining sentences into paragraphs with various linking devices. The activities are quite tightly controlled. This is not to suggest that more creative work is not valid, but it is one of the responsibilities of a coursebook to provide a systematic grounding in the skill. More creative writing is covered in the Practice Book. Work is also done on punctuation, and most of the writing activities are based on real-life tasks, such as writing letters and cards.

Sounds

Pronunciation, stress and intonation work tends to inter-rupt the communicative flow of a lesson, and there is a temptation to leave it out in the interests of maintaining the momentum of an activity sequence. In *Reward* there is work on sounds in most lessons, usually just before the stage where the learners have to use the new structures orally in pairwork or groupwork. At this level, it seems suitable to introduce work beyond the straightforward system of English phonemes, most of which the learners will be able to reproduce accurately because the same phonemes exist in their own language. So activities which focus on stress in words and sentences, and on the implied meaning of certain intonation patterns are included. The model for pronunciation is standard British.

Topics

The main topics proposed by the Threshold Level are covered in *Reward* Intermediate. These include personal identification, house and home, daily life, leisure activities, travel, relations with other people, health, education, shopping, food and drink, geographical location and the environment. On many occasions the words presented in the vocabulary box all belong to a particular word field or topic.

Learner training

Implicit in the overall approach is the development of learner training to encourage learners to take responsibility for their own learning. Examples of this are regular oppor-tunities to use monolingual and bilingual dictionaries, ways of organising vocabulary according to personal categories and inductive grammar work.

Cross-cultural training

Much of the material and activities in *Reward* creates the opportunity for cross-cultural training. Most learners will be using English as a medium of communication with other non-native speakers, and certainly with people of different cultures. Errors of socio-cultural competence are likely to be less easily tolerated than errors of grammar or lexical insufficiency. But it is impossible to give the learners enough specific information about a culture, because it is impossible to predict all the cultural circumstances in which they will use their newly acquired language compet-ence. Information about *sample* cultures, such as Britain and America, as well as non-English speaking ones, is given to allow the learners to compare their own culture with another. This creates opportunities for learners to reflect on their own culture in order to become more aware of the possibility of different attitudes, behaviour, customs, traditions and beliefs in other cultures. In this spirit, cross-cultural training is possible even with groups where the learners all come from the same cultural background. There are interesting and revealing differences between people from the same region or town, or even between friends and members of the same family. Exploring these will help the learners become not merely proficient in the language but competent in the overall aim of communication.

Level and progress

One important principle behind *Reward* is that the learners arrive at intermediate level with very different language abilities and requirements. Some may find the early lessons very easy and will be able to move quickly
on to later lessons. The way *Reward* is structured, with individual lessons of approximately 90 minutes, means that these learners can confirm that they have acquired a certain area of grammar, language function and vocabulary, con-solidate this competence with activities giving practice in the other aspects of the course design, and then move on. Others may find that their previous language competence needs to be reactivated more carefully and slowly. The core teaching lesson in the Student's Book may not provide them with enough practice material to ensure that the given grammar, language functions and vocabulary have been firmly acquired. For these learners, extra practice may be needed and is provided in both the Practice Book (for self-study work) and by the Resource Packs (for class-room work). If learners return to language training at intermediate level after a long period of little or no practice, it is hard to predict quite what they still know. *Reward* is designed to help this kind of learner as much as those who need to confirm that they have already acquired a basic knowledge of English.

Correction

You may need to tell your students your policy on cor-rection. Some may expect you to correct every mistake; others will be hesitant to join in if they are nervous of correction. You need to decide when and how often you want to correct people. Of course, this will depend on the person and the activity, but it might be worth making the distinction between activities which encourage accuracy, in which it is very suitable to provide a certain amount of correction, and activities which focus on fluency, in which it may be better to note down mistakes and give them to the student at a later stage. Another approach may be to encourage accuracy at the beginning of a practice sequence and fluency towards the end. Let them know the general principles. It will create a positive impression even for those who may, at first, disagree with it.

Interest and motivation

Another important principle in the course design has been the intrinsic interest of the materials. Interesting material motivates the learners, and motivated learners acquire the language more effectively. The topics have been carefully selected so that they are interesting to adults and young adults, with a focus on areas which would engage their general leisure-time interests. This is designed to generate what might be described as authentic motivation, the kind of motivation we have when we read a newspaper or watch a television programme. But it is obvious that we cannot motivate all learners all of the time. They may arrive at a potentially motivating lesson with little desire to learn on this particular occasion, perhaps for reasons that have nothing to do with the teacher, the course or the material. It is therefore necessary to introduce tasks which attract what might be described as pedagogic or artificial motiva-tion, tasks which would not usually be performed in real life, but which engage the learner in an artificial but no
less effective way.

Variety of material and language

Despite the enormous amount of research done on language acquisition, no one has come up with a definitive description of how we acquire either our native language or a foreign language which takes account of every language learner or the teaching style of every teacher. Every learner has different interests and different requirements, and every teacher has a different style and approach to what they teach. *Reward* attempts to adopt an approach which appeals to differing styles of learning and teaching. The pivotal role of grammar and vocabulary is reflected in the material, but not at the expense of the development of the skills or pronunciation. An integrated multi-syllabus course design, designed to respond to the broad variety of learners' requirements and teachers' objectives, is at the heart of *Reward's* approach.

RESEARCH

Heinemann ELT is committed to continuing research into coursebook development. Many teachers contributed to the evolution of *Reward* through piloting and reports, and we now want to continue this process of feedback by inviting users of *Reward* – both teachers and students – to tell us about their experience of working with the course. If you or your colleagues have any comments, queries or suggestions, please address them to the Publishing Director, Adult Group, Heinemann ELT, Halley Court, Jordan Hill, Oxford OX2 8EJ or contact your local Heinemann representative.

REWARD

Intermediate

Teacher's Book

Simon Greenall

Heinemann

Map of the Book

Lesson	Grammar and functions	Vocabulary	Skills and sounds
11 *Do it now!* Organisational skills and routine activities	Present perfect (1): *already, yet, still*	Verbs for household actions	**Reading:** reading and answering a questionnaire **Listening:** listening for specific information **Speaking:** talking about domestic activities and personal organisation
12 *London calling* Radio news broadcasts	Present perfect continuous (1) for asking and saying how long	Words connected with news items; politics and military	**Listening:** listening for main ideas **Sounds:** word stress in sentences **Writing:** reconstituting a text **Speaking:** expressing opinions
13 *Fictional heroes never die* Famous characters from fiction	Present perfect simple (2) and present perfect continuous (2)	New words from a passage called *Fictional heroes never die*	**Reading:** reading for main ideas **Speaking:** talking about important events in your life **Writing:** writing a short biography
14 *Twin cities* A view of Prague	Making comparisons	Town features and facilities	**Listening:** inferring **Reading:** reading for specific information **Writing:** writing a description of a town, using linking words *the main reason why, another reason is that, both...and, neither...nor, while, whereas*
15 *I couldn't live without it* Personal possessions	Adjectives (2): order of adjectives	Possessions and objects around the home Compound nouns Noun and adjectives which go together Techniques for dealing with unfamiliar words	**Reading:** reading for main ideas **Sounds:** stress in compound nouns **Speaking:** talking about personal possessions
Progress check lessons 11 – 15	Revision	Adjectives and participles Adjectives which go after the noun	**Sounds:** consonant clusters in end position; linking words in connected speech; stressed words in sentences **Speaking:** describing objects
16 *Do it in style* Style and fashion	Asking for and giving advice; *must* and *should*	Clothes, accessories, appearance Material and colours Techniques for dealing with unfamiliar words	**Reading:** reading for main ideas **Speaking:** talking about fashion **Writing:** writing advice for visitors to your country
17 *Rose Rose* A ghost story by Barry Pain	Making predictions: *may* and *might; going to* and *will*	New words from a story called *Rose Rose*	**Listening:** listening for main ideas; listening for specific information **Speaking:** predicting **Writing:** writing the ending of a story from a different point of view; linking words *although, in spite of* + *-ing*
18 *What do you do for a living?* Jobs and conditions of work	Drawing conclusions; *must, can't, might, could;* describing impressions	Jobs Adjectives to describe personal and professional qualities	**Speaking:** talking about your job or your ideal job **Sounds:** stressed syllables in words; intonation when disagreeing **Listening:** listening for specific information **Reading:** understanding text organisation
19 *Guided tours* Pilgrimage to Santiago de Compostela	Talking about obligation, permission and prohibition	Religion and tourism	**Reading:** reading for main ideas; inferring **Sounds:** strong and weak forms of *can, have to* and *must* **Writing:** a description of rules in your country
20 *How unfair can you get?* Emotional reactions	Talking about ability and possibility: *can, could, be able to*	Compound adjectives	**Speaking:** talking about personal qualities **Listening:** predicting; listening for main ideas; listening for detail; listening for specific information **Writing:** re-telling the story from notes and from the listening activity
Progress check lessons 16 – 20	Revision	Multi-part verbs: phrasal verbs and prepositional verbs with objects	**Sounds:** different ways of pronouncing the letter *a;* linking words in connected speech; consonant clusters in initial position **Speaking:** talking about unlikely statements **Writing:** writing statements which must be, might be and can't be true

Lesson	Grammar and functions	Vocabulary	Skills and sounds
21 *Cinema classics* Films	Adverbs (2): formation; giving opinions; emphasising	Types of films Adjectives to describe opinions	**Listening:** listening for specific information; listening for main ideas **Sounds:** strong intonation for emphasising an opinion **Writing:** inserting words; writing the plot of a classic film **Speaking:** talking about classic films
22 *Wild and beautiful* Animal conservation	Adverbs (3): position of adverbs and adverbial phrases	Animals	**Reading:** reading for main ideas; evaluating a text **Speaking:** talking about environmental changes in the world **Writing:** writing about something which has changed with linking words *ago, then, today, in ...years' time*
23 *Valentine* A poem	Reported speech (1): statements	Love symbols Techniques for dealing with unfamiliar words Adjectives to describe personal characteristics	**Reading:** reading for specific information **Listening:** inferring; listening for main ideas **Sounds:** reciting a poem **Speaking:** talking about romantic things, people and places **Writing:** writing a poem
24 *Medium wave* The media	Reported speech (2): questions	Newspapers, television and radio	**Listening:** listening for specific information **Writing:** writing a report of an interview; linking words *the reason for this, because, another reason for this, besides* **Speaking:** talking about the media
25 *A cup of tea* A short story by Katherine Mansfield	Reported speech (3): reporting verbs	New words from a story called *A cup of tea*	**Speaking:** predicting **Reading:** predicting; reading for main ideas **Writing:** rewriting the story from another point of view
Progress check lessons 21 – 25	Revision	Multi-part verbs: phrasal verbs without objects and phrasal prepositional verbs	**Sounds:** different ways of pronouncing the letter *e*; silent consonants; stress when correcting someone **Speaking:** talking about yourself; responding to others
26 *Eat your heart out... in the USA* American regional cooking	Giving instructions and special advice	Food Ways of preparing food, ways of cooking, kitchen equipment	**Speaking:** talking about typical food from your country or region **Reading:** reading for specific information; reacting to a text **Listening:** listening for specific information; understanding text organisation
27 *Home thoughts from abroad* Holiday postcards	Defining relative clauses	Holidays	**Speaking:** talking about holiday postcards **Reading:** reading for main ideas; linking ideas **Sounds:** pauses in relative clauses **Listening:** listening for main ideas **Writing:** writing postcards
28 *Local produce* Things grown and made in Britain	The passive	Manufactured and natural products Words which go together Techniques for dealing with unfamiliar words	**Reading:** reading for main ideas **Speaking:** talking about typical food, drink or products of your town, region or country **Writing:** writing about typical food, drink or products
29 *Just what we're looking for!* Looking for somewhere to live	Verb patterns (2): *need* + *-ing* and passive infinitive; causative constructions with *have* and *get*; reflexive pronouns	Adjectives to describe things which go wrong with a house Furniture and fittings Jobs Verbs for household maintenance	**Reading:** reading for main ideas **Speaking:** discussing if you are houseproud; talking about homes
30 *Sporting chance* New rules for old sports	Verb patterns (3): *make* and *let*; infinitive constructions after adjectives	Sports and sports equipment Words which go together	**Reading:** inferring **Listening:** listening for main ideas **Sounds:** stressed words in sentences **Speaking:** talking about sport
Progress check lessons 26 – 30	Revision	Verbs and nouns which go together Words which are sometimes confused	**Sounds:** different ways of pronouncing the letter *i* **Reading:** understanding text organisation **Writing:** inserting words and sentences

Lesson	Grammar and functions	Vocabulary	Skills and sounds
31 *I never leave home without it* Useful objects and equipment	Zero conditional: *in case*	Personal possessions	**Listening:** listening for main ideas **Sounds:** syllable stress **Reading:** reading for main ideas **Speaking:** talking about the things you always take with you
32 *Politely but firmly* Letters Complaining about a new car	Describing a sequence of events (3): *as soon as, when* and *after* for future events	Parts of a car	**Speaking:** talking about making complaints **Reading:** reading for main ideas **Listening:** listening for main ideas **Writing:** writing a letter of complaint
33 *Superhints* Practical household advice	Verb patterns (4): infinitive of purpose; *by* + *-ing*; giving advice; *if* clauses	Household objects and actions	**Reading:** reading for specific information **Sounds:** different pronunciation of vowels and diphthongs; weak forms in connected speech **Listening:** listening for specific information **Writing:** writing household advice
34 *The green tourist* The effects of tourism on the environment	First conditional	New words from a passage called *Are you a green tourist?* Words which go together	**Reading:** reading for main ideas; inferring **Sounds:** /ɪ/; stress and intonation in first conditional sentences **Listening:** listening for specific information **Speaking:** talking about the effects of tourism
35 *Lost in the Pacific* The story of Amelia Earhart	Past perfect simple and continuous	New words from a passage about Amelia Earhart	**Reading:** reading for main ideas; understanding text organisation **Writing:** writing a paragraph about an unsolved mystery
Progress check lessons 31 – 35	Revision	English words borrowed from other languages Words which go in pairs Antonyms	**Sounds:** different ways of pronouncing the letter *o*; syllable stress **Speaking:** talking about true and false information about Britain **Listening:** listening for main ideas
36 *What's your advice?* Letters to a problem page	Second conditional; giving advice	Relationships	**Reading:** reading for main ideas **Sounds:** linking words in connected speech **Listening:** listening for main ideas **Writing:** writing a letter of advice
37 *You should have been here last week* A visit to Hong Kong	Past modal verbs (1): *should have*	Tourism in Hong Kong Techniques for dealing with unfamiliar words	**Reading:** reading for main ideas; inferring **Listening:** listening for main ideas; listening for detail **Speaking:** talking about something you did wrong and which you regret
38 *Now you see me, now you don't* Strange and supernatural incidents	Past modals (2): *may have, might have, could have, must have, can't have*	New words from three stories about strange incidents	**Reading:** understanding text organisation; inserting phrases **Speaking:** telling stories; speculating
39 *Making the grade* Education in Britain and the USA	Expressing wishes and regrets	Education Subjects that are studied at school or college	**Listening:** listening for specific information **Sounds:** /d/; intonation in sentences with *if only* **Speaking:** talking about important events in your educational career **Writing:** writing a description of the education system in your country; linking words *like* and *unlike*
40 *The man who was everywhere* A thriller by Edward D. Hoch	Third conditional	New words from a story called *The man who was everywhere*	**Reading:** understanding text organisation; understanding a writer's style **Listening:** listening for main ideas **Speaking:** predicting; discussing what you would have done **Writing:** rewriting the story from a different point of view
Progress check lessons 36 – 40	Revision	Colloquial language Idiomatic expressions Techniques for dealing with unfamiliar words	**Sounds:** different ways of pronouncing the letter *u*; silent letters; linking words in connected speech **Reading:** understanding text organisation **Speaking:** reacting to a story

1

GENERAL COMMENTS

Course design

This lesson contains presentation and practice of most of the main syllabus strands to be found in *Reward* Intermediate: *Vocabulary, Grammar, Functions, Sounds, Reading, Listening* and *Speaking* (the other main syllabus strand is *Writing*) and it is therefore a fairly typical lesson in its range and diversity of activities.

Starting the course

This lesson concerns the language and behaviour required for effective teaching and learning in the classroom. Use the opportunity to make sure the students get to know each other, and to introduce them to any rules you may want them to follow, such as if they can smoke or how punctual you expect them to be. The underlying theme is developing consideration for each other in the classroom.

VOCABULARY AND READING

1 Aim: to present or revise some vocabulary used for describing people and their backgrounds.
- It is likely that students will have come across these words already in a previous class. In this case, prepare some information about yourself using only the words and phrases from the box which they may have difficulty with. Write this information on the board.

- Ask one or two students to choose a word and use the word in sentences about themselves. If your students do not know each other, or if you don't know them very well, this is a chance to find out about each other.

- Ask the students to choose five or six words and write sentences about themselves.

2 Aim: to practise using the vocabulary in the box, and to find out about each other.
- Ask the students to work in pairs and to show each other their sentences. If possible, ask them to go round different people in the class to share their information.

- Find out if anyone can remember any interesting, amusing or surprising information about each other.

- Ask the students to group the vocabulary in the box according to any words which go together.

3 Aim: to present or revise vocabulary used for talking about language learning and the classroom.
- Ask the students to look at the words in the box and to check they understand them. If anyone asks the meaning of a word, see if other students can explain, perhaps by using examples taken from the textbook or the classroom.

- Ask the students to underline the verbs. You may like to point out that some words are both nouns and verbs.

4 Aim: to practise using the words in the vocabulary box; to present the main headings of *Reward*.
- Point out that there are seven main headings for the activities in *Reward* and that they are signposts to show clearly what the students are doing at a given point in a lesson. Ask them to complete the instructions with words from the box. The sentences all come from the first ten lessons of *Reward* Intermediate, and they will find the answers by looking under the headings in brackets at the end of each sentence.

Answers
1 Read the passage and match the names with the paragraphs. (READING)
2 Here are some new words from the story. Check you understand what they mean. (VOCABULARY)
3 Complete these sentences with *who, where* or *which*. (GRAMMAR)
4 Listen and underline anything in the conversation that is different from what you hear. (LISTENING)
5 Listen and say these words aloud. (SOUNDS)
6 Write notes/sentences in answer to these questions. (WRITING)
7 Work in pairs. Ask and say what you like doing. (SPEAKING)

5 Aim: to read and answer a questionnaire; to develop a positive attitude towards learning and a spirit of co-operation; to present transactional language for the classroom; to suggest some learner training techniques; to focus on polite forms.
- This activity is designed to explore attitudes and behaviour towards the teacher and other students in the classroom. You may find it helpful at this early stage in the course to establish some ground rules concerning co-operation, mutual respect and positive learning behaviour. Ask students to read the questionnaire and to think about their answers. Try to discourage them from asking about the meaning of individual words, as there has already been quite a lot of vocabulary work in this lesson so far. If they insist, check if other students can answer any vocabulary difficulties, and if not, say that you will explain to the whole group the meaning of five words only, and that they should choose these words carefully.

- Wait until *Listening* activity 2 before checking their answers.

- Take this opportunity to explain that, in English, it is customary to be as polite as possible even in transactional situations such as buying a bus ticket or asking a very basic favour. When the students use English, they may not wish to adopt the customs and behaviour of native English speakers, but in this case they should be aware that in certain circumstances they may be considered impolite.

LISTENING

1 Aim: to practise listening for main ideas.

● 📼 Explain that Gail, the English teacher on the tape, is listening to Tony, a French student, answering the questionnaire. The reading activity will have prepared the students for listening, so ask them to listen for the main idea of the speaker's answers.

> **Answers**
> 1 c 2 b 3 b 4 a 5 b 6 a 7 c 8 b

2 Aim: to practise speaking about behaviour and attitudes in the classroom.

● Ask the students to work in pairs and to discuss Tony's answers. Spend some time talking about why the other choices are not acceptable. Dissuade them from discussing their own answers at this point.

GRAMMAR

1 Aim: to focus on word order in questions.

● Ask the students to read the information in the grammar box.

● Explain to the students that mistakes in word order in questions are very common, even among good intermediate students. The most common one is the placing of the verb in indirect questions (for example, *Could you tell me what is your name?*). Ask them to put the words in the right order.

> **Answers**
> 1 Where were you born?
> 2 What nationality are you?
> 3 Could you tell me what your name is?
> 4 Could you repeat that, please?
> 5 Would you mind speaking more slowly, please?
> 6 I wonder if you could tell me what 'spare-time' means?

2 Aim: to focus on asking questions and asking for and giving help in the classroom.

● Write on the board, two or three names, dates and places which are important to you. Think about where you were born, where you lived as a child, the name of your best friend or partner, the year you changed school or place of work. Elicit questions about yourself, such as *Did you start school in 1975? Did you live in Lyon?* and answer them truthfully *No, I didn't* or *Yes, I did*.

● Ask the students to do the same, writing down four or five pieces of information about themselves.

3 Aim: to practise asking questions.

● Ask students to work together asking and answering questions using the information they wrote in activity 2 as prompts. Go round and check that everyone is asking suitable and correct questions.

4 Aim: to practise asking for and giving help in the classroom.

● This activity is designed to help the students check their answers to the questionnaire and to practise using the language presented in it.

SOUNDS

Aim: to expose the students to polite and unfriendly intonation; to give practise in using polite and friendly intonation.

● Ask the students to read the questions in *Grammar* activity 1 and to guess who might be saying them and where.

● Remind the students that English intonation can reveal a great deal about the speaker's attitude and behaviour. The same sentence can have quite a different meaning depending on the intonation it has. Ask them if their own languages use intonation in the same way.

● 📼 Explain that some of the sentences they will hear will be friendly and polite and others will be unfriendly. Play the tape and ask them to tick the friendly-sounding questions.

● Ask them say the questions aloud, using polite and friendly intonation.

> **Answers**
> 1 (polite) 2 (unfriendly) 3 (polite) 4 (unfriendly)
> 5 (polite) 6 (polite)

SPEAKING

1 Aim: to compare behaviour and attitudes in the classroom; to examine acceptable and unacceptable questions.

● Use this activity to encourage the students to think about the kind of questions which may be more or less acceptable to ask people. In the Far East, for example, it is not usual to use first names except between members of the same family. In parts of Africa and the Middle East, it may be impolite to ask questions about one's family. In Europe, it is not common to ask people their age or how much they earn.

2 Aim: to practise asking and answering questions about yourself and your colleagues.

● This activity gives the students a final opportunity to practise asking questions and giving personal information about themselves.

2

GENERAL COMMENTS

Present tenses

The grammar focus of this lesson is the present tenses. Students will have already seen some of the different uses of the present simple and continuous tenses, so this lesson presents them contrastively. If you think that they have already learnt to use these tenses successfully, shift your teaching focus away from the grammar and onto another aspect of the course design, such as listening or writing.

Use of photos

The photos in *Reward* are generally chosen not just because they generate discussion but also because they stimulate the students' motivation by being attractive to look at and by contributing to the appeal of the two-page spread of the textbook lesson. If the material in *Reward* was presented as solid blocks of text, the students' motivation to learn and to enjoy the learning experience might be compromised. In each lesson there are some questions which can be used to exploit the photos, generally as a way of introducing the lesson's theme.

Possible questions

What can you see in the photo?
Is it in the town or the countryside?
What country do you think the station is in?
What time of day is it?
Do you think it is always like this?
When do you think the photo was taken?

VOCABULARY AND LISTENING

1 Aim: to prepare for listening by focusing first on the background noise.
- Ask the students to suggest as many words as possible which are connected with travel by train, and write them on the board.

- Explain to the students that it is sometimes difficult to hear what people are saying if there is a lot of background noise. However, this noise may in fact contain a great deal of information about the context of what is being said. This activity is designed to isolate the background noise so it can be analysed before the students begin listening to the interviews. It also helps them prepare for listening by thinking about the context.

- ▣ Play the background noise and ask them to guess in which three places the interviews will take place. Do not elicit answers at this stage as students should discuss their answers using the words in activity 2.

> **Answers**
> First situation: on the platform
> Second situation: at the main entrance
> Third situation: at the ticket office

2 Aim: to prepare for listening by thinking about the context; to present some vocabulary.
- Encourage the students to be as inventive as possible when answering the questions. There are no correct answers, but a creative group will imagine a whole scenario based on the sounds they can hear.

- Check that students understand all the words in the vocabulary box, and encourage them to use them when they're imagining other details about the background noise. If there are any words they don't understand, try to find other students who can explain them before explaining their meaning yourself.

3 Aim: to practise listening for main ideas; to prepare for practise of the use of the present tenses.
- ▣ Tell the students they are going to hear three interviews with people at Grand Central Station in New York. Play the tape and ask them to put the number of the interview in the box in which they hear each phrase.

- They will use these answers in *Grammar* activities 1 and 2.

> **Answers**
>
> | | |
> |---|---|
> | get back home | Interview 3 |
> | spend Christmas with grandchildren | Interview 3 |
> | wait for a train | Interview 1 |
> | have a cup of coffee | Interview 1 |
> | take the train | Interview 3 |
> | walk to work | Interview 2 |
> | have a rehearsal | Interview 2 |
> | take a cab | Interview 2 |
> | work for an advertising agency | Interview 1 |
> | play the cello | Interview 2 |
> | teach music | Interview 2 |
> | work in Wall Street | Interview 3 |

- You may want to mention that the people speak with a typical New York accent. Do the students notice the difference between this accent and the English accent of Gail in Lesson 1 *Listening and speaking*?

- Check also that everyone has understood what each person's job is.

4 Aim: to check that students have correctly completed activity 3.
- ▣ This activity gives the students the opportunity to hear the interviews a second time. You may want to stop after each interview. However, it is advisable to avoid explaining every word they don't understand. Play the tape again.

GRAMMAR

1 Aim: to focus on the difference between the present simple and the present continuous.

● Ask the students to read the information about the present simple and the present continuous in the grammar box.

● Ask the students to answer the questions. You may like to do this orally, but it can be done individually in writing as well.

● You may like to ask the students to check their answers in pairs, and then check them with the whole class.

> **Answers**
> **Fran Ramirez**
> 1 Fran Ramirez works for an advertising agency.
> 2 She's having a cup of coffee and something to eat.
> 3 She walks to work from Grand Central.
> 4 No, she isn't. She's having a cup of coffee.
> **Henry North**
> 1 Henry North usually teaches music.
> 2 He's playing cello for the orchestra at the Met.
> 3 He usually walks.
> 4 He's taking a cab.

2 Aim: to focus on the use of the present continuous for a definite arrangement in the future.

● Ask the students to do this activity in writing, because if the questions occurred in natural speech, it would be normal to give short answers. Here, practice in writing the full form of the present continuous is required. Contractions are acceptable, although you can explain that they are less common in formal situations.

● You may like to ask them to check their answers in pairs, orally before doing this with the whole class.

> **Answers**
> 1 They're spending Christmas in Chicago.
> 2 They're taking the three o'clock train.
> 3 They're spending Christmas with their grandchildren, then they're going to Toronto and spending a few days with friends.
> 4 They're arriving at nine in the morning.

3 Aim: to practise using the present simple and the present continuous; to practise writing sentences giving personal information.

● Point to the six uses of the present simple and continuous in the grammar box. Ask the students to write sentences about themselves or their town, each sentence illustrating one of these uses.

● Ask the students to work in pairs and to show each other their sentences.

● Ask the students to read aloud their sentences to the rest of the class. Which is the most interesting, amusing or unusual piece of information?

● You may like to ask the students to do this activity for homework.

WRITING

1 Aim: to practise reading for specific information.

● Explain that the letter is from the couple who were interviewed last in *Vocabulary and listening* activity 3, to their son and daughter-in-law. Check everyone understands that the day of travel (and the day the interviews took place is Thursday 23 December). Ask them to read it and make a list of their arrangements.

> **Answers**
> | | |
> |---|---|
> | Thursday 23 | Leave New York |
> | Friday 24 | Arrive Chicago |
> | Saturday 25 | Spend Christmas with Maisie and Tom |
> | Monday 27 | Leave Chicago, go to Toronto, stay with Gary and Holly |
> | Friday 31 | Return to New York |

2 Aim: to focus on the layout of letters.

● It's important to stress that the layout of letters can vary between British and American usage. You may like to explain that students can still lay out their letters according to the usage in their country, but that they must not assume that the salutations and endings can be simply translated from their own language into English. This activity simply makes the students aware of the common conventions in English for writing personal letters. Mention that more formal letters have different conventions and will be discussed in Lesson 32.

> **Answers**
> 1 The address at the top is the person writing the letter.
> 2 Write *Dear* and then the name(s) of the person(s) you're writing to.
> 3 The date goes under the address.
> 4 You write *Love* or *Best wishes, Kind regards. Yours sincerely* is used to finish a formal letter to someone you know, *Yours faithfully* for someone you don't know.

3 Aim: to prepare for activity 4 which practises using the present continuous for future arrangements.

● Ask the students to write down their arrangements for next week. If an important holiday, such as Christmas or Easter is near, they can write about their holiday arrangements. Alternatively, you can suggest that their arrangements are as exotic or exciting as they can imagine. You can write your own arrangements on the board as a model, for example, *Monday lunch with the President, dinner with Madonna...*

4 Aim: to practise letter writing; to practise using the present continuous for future arrangements.

● Ask the students to think of a friend, perhaps someone in the classroom, and to use their notes to write them a letter talking about their arrangements. Point out that the letter in 1 can be used as a model.

● You may like to ask the students to do this activity for homework.

3

GENERAL COMMENTS

Cross-cultural awareness

An important syllabus strand in the course design of *Reward* is socio-cultural competence, or developing cross-cultural awareness. Even if you speak a language fluently, effective communication may be impaired for cultural reasons, and in general, people are less tolerant of cultural *faux pas* than they are of grammatical mistakes or vocabulary deficiencies. In *Reward* there is a great deal of material about different cultures, which encourages the students to make comparisons with their own cultures. This cross-cultural material sometimes deals with behaviour and attitudes, and sometimes with customs and traditions, as in this lesson. It is above all designed to be interesting and motivating, but should also help students to learn about other cultures and about their own.

Reading

Many of the passages in *Reward* Intermediate have vocabulary which is above the immediate level of the students. This is intentional as it will help them prepare for a similar situation which may occur in real life. The students should also be encouraged to guess the meaning of unfamiliar words rather than ask the teacher for help or look the word up in the dictionary. It should be explained that it is not necessary to find out or write down the meaning of every item of new vocabulary. Point out that the vocabulary which is most useful in a given lesson is listed in the vocabulary box.

Jigsaw reading

A jigsaw-reading activity involves the students working in pairs, each one reading a different passage on a similar theme. They then exchange information about each other's passage, and thus practise speaking as well. The activity is an efficient way of creating an information gap, in which Student A has information that Student B doesn't have, and vice versa.

VOCABULARY AND SPEAKING

1 **Aim: to present vocabulary used to talk about wedding ceremonies; to pre-teach some new vocabulary to be found in the reading passages.**
   ● Explain that the theme of the lesson is wedding ceremonies. Ask students if they have been to a wedding ceremony recently and if so, what happened.

   ● Ask the students to work in pairs and to decide which words they can use to describe the preparation, the ceremony and the celebrations for a wedding. If anyone does not understand any of the words, find out if other students can explain them before doing so yourself.

2 **Aim: to practise speaking.**
   ● Ask the students to talk about wedding ceremonies in their own countries. Ask them to describe the sequence of events in a traditional ceremony in as much detail as possible.

READING

1 **Aim: to read and extract the main ideas.**
   ● Ask the students to read the passage and to find out why it is called *All dressed in red* and in which country the wedding ceremony takes place.

   > **Answer**
   > The Hindu bride wears red on her wedding day.

   ● Encourage the students to think about the most interesting or surprising facts in the passage, and to compare Hindu wedding customs with weddingcustoms in their own country.

2 **Aim: to read for specific information.**
   ● Ask the students to read the passage again and to look for details about the different points.

   > **Answers**
   > See activity 4.

3 **Aim: to practise reading for specific information.**
   ● Explain that this is a jigsaw reading activity, which involves one student reading one passage and the other reading another passage on the same topic. Make sure everyone knows whether they are Student A or Student B, and that they should not look for or read the other student's passage. Show them where the Communication activities are (at the back of the book from page 98) and ask them to read their passages.

   ● Correct the students' answers in activity 4.

4 **Aim: to practise speaking.**
   ● This next stage of the jigsaw-reading activity encourages the students to exchange information about each others' text. Ask them to work in pairs again, and to talk about the points mentioned in activity 2.

   > **Answers**
   > **Hindu**
   > preparations: the holy man studies the horoscopes
   > presents: jewels
   > dress: henna on hands and feet, sari
   > reception: feast of food and drink, bride and groom
   >   share their meal
   > ceremony: mark of red paste, face covered with veil
   >
   > **Moslem**
   > preparations: groom's family visits bride's family to
   >   ask for the bride's hand; then they drink coffee
   >   and talk about the arrangements
   > presents: gold and jewellery
   > dress: the bride is dressed in white
   > reception: two separate parties, then bride and
   >   groom sit on stage and open presents
   > ceremony: two ceremonies, only the groom attends
   >   the Moslem ceremony, the bride is repesented by
   >   a sister or friend.

Chinese

preparations: presents from groom's family to bride's family, horoscopes

presents: gifts of pork, chickens, candles and clothing to bride's family; red packets containing gold, jewellery or money from the guests

dress: bride and groom in silk

reception: lunch or dinner of fifteen courses, with entertainment by a singer and band

ceremony: three ceremonies

FUNCTIONS AND GRAMMAR

1 Aim: to focus on the use of *before/after* + *-ing* **or subject + verb.**

● Ask the students to read the passage again and to underline all the *before/after* constructions.

● Ask one or two students to read out a few examples of the construction. Make sure they include a similar number of *-ing* and subject + verb examples.

● Ask the students to read the information on describing a sequence of events in the functions and grammar box.

2 Aim: to practise using *before/after* + **subject + verb to describe a sequence of events.**

● Explain that the students should join the two sentences. First they must decide which event comes first, and to use *before/after* + subject + verb at the beginning of the first sentence. They can do this orally in pairs, or in writing. Check the answers with the whole class.

Answers
1 **After** the Hindu holy man checks the horoscope, he chooses the wedding day.
2 **After** friends and relatives paint the Hindu bride's hands and feet, she puts on her sari.
3 **Before** the groom's relatives cover the bride and groom with a veil, they decorate the bride with jewels.
4 **Before** the Moslem couple celebrate their wedding together, the groom attends a religious ceremony.
5 **After** they arrive at the reception, they receive the wedding presents.
6 **After** the matchmaker takes a present to the Chinese bride, the groom can propose to his bride.
7 **After** they agree to the marriage, they check the couple's horoscopes.
8 **Before** they ask the gods for their help, the matchmaker makes sure the signs are good.

3 Aim: to practise using *before/after* + *-ing* **to describe a sequence of events.**

● Ask the students to decide which sentence can be rewritten with *before/after* + *-ing*. Remind them if necessary that only the sentences which have the same subject in both clauses can be written with *before/after* + *-ing*.

4 Aim: to focus on the use of *during* **and** *for*.

● Ask the students to read the information on *during* and *for* in the functions and grammar box, and then to complete the sentences.

Answers
1 **During** the ceremony, they exchange rings.
2 The reception may last **for** two days.
3 Preparations go on **for** several months.
4 **During** the reception the couple receives presents.
5 She wears the red mark **for** the rest of her married life.
6 The holy man studies the horoscopes **during** this period.

SPEAKING AND WRITING

1 Aim: to practise speaking; to prepare for describing a sequence of events in activity 2.

● Ask the students to work in groups of two or three and to talk about weddings in their country or countries. Encourage them to talk about alternative kinds of weddings as well as traditional weddings.

● Find out if the students think marriage is as important or popular as it was fifty years ago.

2 Aim: to prepare for writing about a sequence of events.

● Ask the students to make notes on each stage, both before and after the main ceremony itself. You may like to tell them that in Britain, you either get married in a church or in a registry office, but there is no need to do both.

3 Aim: to practise using *before/after* + *-ing* **or subject + verb.**

● Ask the students to join their notes with *before/after* + *-ing* or subject + verb constructions and *during/for* constructions. They can do this on their own or in their groups. Go round and check they are doing this correctly.

● You may like to ask the students to do this activity for homework.

4

GENERAL COMMENTS

Listening

Many learners find listening to be the most difficult skill to develop, usually because, unlike the other receptive skill, reading, they are not in control of the rate of delivery of the information they're listening to. Not surprisingly, this creates nervousness and a lack of confidence in the students. Furthermore, because listening comprehension is often practised with material on audio tape, the students are deprived of important clues as to the meaning of the passage. In real life, the students will constantly be exposed to language which is more complex than their current level. It is important to prepare the students for this situation in the classroom. Even though the level of language in the listening material will vary, the tasks in *Reward* Intermediate are carefully graded. Encourage the students to listen for the main ideas, to perform the task set and not to worry about words which they don't understand or recognise. It is important not to play the tape bit by bit, stopping after each line, as this will encourage students to believe they should try and understand every word.

VOCABULARY AND READING

1 Aim: to present the words in the vocabulary box.
- Explain that you can use the adjectives in the box to describe your opinions about something, especially things you like and dislike doing.

- Check everyone understands the meaning of the words by asking them to put them in order from positive to negative. Ask them to choose the two most extreme adjectives (for example, *terrific/wonderful/brilliant - dreadful/awful*) and write them on the board with a large gap between them.

- Draw a line between the two extremes and ask them to suggest where *OK* and *all right* can go. Make sure they suggest these adjective phrases go roughly in the middle.

- Ask them to suggest where the others can go. If there's little difference between adjectives, put them on top of each other.

> **Possible answers**
> **positive:** terrific, brilliant, superb, wonderful, great, exciting, fun, relaxing, nice
> **neutral:** all right, OK
> **negative:** dull, boring, dreadful, terrible, awful

2 Aim: to present some new vocabulary for spare time activities; to practise using the vocabulary presented in activity 1.
- Ask the students *Do you like watching television? Do you like playing football?* etc.

- Ask the students to work in pairs and to choose an adjective from the box in 1 to describe how they feel about the activities. Elicit other leisure activities and ask other students for their opinions.

3 Aim: to practise reading for main ideas.
- Tell the students that the passage will explain what a *couch potato* is. The multiple choice definitions are designed to help them check they have understood the passage. Ask them to read the passage and choose the best definition. Try to avoid answering too many questions about vocabulary at this stage. The task is designed to help them read for main ideas.

> **Answer 2**

4 Aim: to practise using the vocabulary presented in activity 2; to practise speaking.
- Check if there any major vocabulary problems. If there are, tell the class that you will help them with five difficult words, and see if other members of the class can explain the meaning before you have to.

- Encourage the class to discuss how energetic the activities in the box in 2 are, and to give them a score from 1 (= lazy), to 10 (= energetic).

LISTENING

1 Aim: to practise listening for main ideas.
- Explain that you are going to play nine short interviews in which people talk about what they like doing in their free time. Remind students that there may be some difficult words, but that it is not necessary to understand everything.

- 🔲 Play the tape and ask them to put the number of the speaker by the things each person likes doing.

> **Answers**
> Speaker 1: do it yourself
> Speaker 2: playing and watching football
> Speaker 3: entertaining and going to restaurants
> Speaker 4: going shopping
> Speaker 5: watching cricket
> Speaker 6: going to nightclubs
> Speaker 7: fishing
> Speaker 8: gardening
> Speaker 9: watching television

2 Aim: to interpret the interviews.
- Ask the students to read the definition of a *couch potato* again and to decide which speaker in the interviews it might be used to describe.

> **Possible answer**
> Speaker 9

FUNCTIONS AND GRAMMAR

1 Aim: to present or revise ways of talking about likes and dislikes.

● Ask the students to read the information in the functions and grammar box.

● Write on the board sentences saying how you feel about doing the washing, ironing etc, for example, *I detest doing the washing, I don't mind doing the ironing* etc.

● Ask the students to write sentences saying how they feel about the activities mentioned. If the structures are not new to them, you may like to do this orally with the whole class.

● If the students have written sentences, you may like to ask one or two to read them aloud.

2 Aim: to focus on the difference between *to* and *-ing*.

● This distinction may be new to intermediate learners, so you may want to check everyone has understood it. Ask them to choose the best verb pattern. You can do this orally with the whole class.

Answers
1 I like to go to the dentist every six months. (because it's a good idea).
2 She likes getting home before it's dark. *OR* She likes to get home before it's dark. (because it's a good idea, but doesn't necessarily enjoy doing so).
3 She likes visiting his parents. (She enjoys it) *OR* She likes to visit his parents. (because it's a good idea, but doesn't necessarily enjoy doing so).
4 He likes to do the washing on Mondays.

● Check the students answers by asking *Is it a good idea?* or *Do you really enjoy it?* to establish the key concepts behind the distinction.

3 Aim: to present or revise adverbs and adverbial phrases of frequency.

● Most intermediate learners will know *sometimes, usually* and *often* but the position of these adverbs in a sentence may be new to them, as will the more complex adverbial phrases of frequency. Ask the students to write sentences saying how often they do the activities. Encourage them to use the more complex phrases if you think the simple ones are well-known to them.

● Check the answers orally with the group as a whole. Make sure the adverb goes in the right position.

SPEAKING AND WRITING

1 Aim: to practise speaking; to prepare for speaking and writing in activities 2 and 3.

● Ask the students to find out if there are any couch potatoes in the class. Ask them to list five favourite hobbies and leisure activities. Encourage them to think of as many different activities as possible.

● Ask the students to work in groups and to agree on a score from 1 to 10 for the different activities.

● Ask the students to add up their individual scores. Does the definition of a couch potato in *Vocabulary and reading* apply to the person with the lowest score?

2 Aim: to practise talking about likes and dislikes.

● Ask the students to go round talking to people about their likes and dislikes. Encourage them to work with people they don't know so well. Suggest that they make a few notes as they go round.

3 Aim: to practise writing about likes and dislikes.

● Ask the students to use their notes to write a paragraph about three or four people's likes and dislikes. Suggest that they use the example as a model for their paragraphs. Encourage them to use the linking devices as suggested.

● You may like to ask the students to do this activity for homework.

5

GENERAL COMMENTS

Adjectives ending in -ed and -ing

It is very common for intermediate learners to confuse adjectives formed from present and past participles. The past participle adjective is passive in meaning and usually refers to a feeling. The present participle adjective is active in meaning and usually refers to the person or thing which causes the feeling.

Question tags

Question tags are used by British speakers of English and less often, or not at all, by other native speakers. Many learners who have an equivalent way of putting a short question at the end of a statement, such as the French and Germans, may use the wrong verb in the English question tag. The rule is that a suitable auxiliary verb is used in the question tag, with an affirmative tag for a negative statement and a negative tag for an affirmative statement. Some students may also answer a question tag with *yes*, when they mean *no*, and vice versa. For example, if you answer *You don't enjoy the sunshine, do you?* with *yes* it means *Yes, I do enjoy the sunshine*. If you answer the same question with *no* it means *No, I don't enjoy the sunshine*. The final difficulty is that in English the meaning can change according to the intonation, as the grammar box explains.

Topics

Listening to British and American music may be a major source of motivation to learn English, particularly for young adult learners, and it is important to exploit this source of motivation as much as possible. However, not every song allows close attention in class – the latest hit by the most fashionable performer may be incomprehensible or unsuitable in its vocabulary load. It might be possible to put more suitable material into the textbook, but by the time the lesson is used in class, the song may be out-of-date. This lesson creates the opportunity to talk about music, but without using material that motivates because of its contemporary impact. You may like to supplement this lesson by asking students to suggest songs to play in this lesson and by exploiting their language potential.

VOCABULARY

1 **Aim: to present the vocabulary in the box.**

● Ask the students to think of as many types of music as possible and write them on the board.

● Ask the students to check the list with the words in the vocabulary box. Do they know of performers who play the types of music in the box or on the board?

● 🔊 Play the tape and ask the students to put the number of each piece by the type of music.

Answers
1 folk
2 classical
3 jazz
4 pop
5 reggae
6 techno

● Some of the types of music may no longer be popular when you do this lesson. Ask the students to suggest other, more fashionable types of music.

2 **Aim: to present the vocabulary in the box; to present adjectives which can be used in the -ed and the -ing form.**

● Encourage the students to use the adjectives in the box to describe how they feel about the different types of music, pieces of music and performers. This activity will also give you an indication of their interests and help you evaluate the potential success of certain types of music if you want to supplement the textbook and Resource Pack material with songs.

3 **Aim: to focus on adjectives which come from verbs.**

● Explain that some adjectives come from verbs and will be either present or past participles. Ask the students to say the verb the adjectives come from.

Answers
Adjectives from verbs: amusing, boring, depressing, exciting, interesting, irritating, moving, relaxing, thrilling

● You may like to ask the students to write sentences to describe their feelings about the types of music in activity 1 using the verbs.

READING

1 **Aim: to react to a text.**

● Ask the students to read the speakers' opinions about music and to decide if they agree with them.

● Ask the students to work in pairs and to talk about their reactions to the opinions. How many people in the class agree or disagree with each one?

2 **Aim: to read for specific information; to practise inferring; to check comprehension.**

● The statements are a reformulation of what the speakers said, and the students' task is to evaluate whether the statements are accurate or not. This is designed to help them practise reading between the lines, and to check they have understood.

Answers
1 True
2 True
3 The passage doesn't say
4 True
5 True
6 The passage doesn't say
7 True

GRAMMAR

1 **Aim: to focus on adjectives ending in -ed and -ing.**

● Ask the students to read the information about adjectives ending in -ed and -ing and question tags in the grammar box.

● Ask the students to complete the sentences with adjectives ending in -ed and -ing . You can do this activity orally.

Answers
1 boring
2 excited
3 embarrassing
4 relaxed
5 thrilling
6 depressing

2 **Aim: to focus on question tags.**

● Ask the students to complete the sentences with question tags. It may be simpler to do this activity orally with the whole class.

Answers
1 aren't you?
2 is it?
3 doesn't she?
4 does he?
5 haven't they?
6 don't you?

SOUNDS

Aim: to focus on the intonation of question tags.

● 🔲 Remind the students that in the grammar box, they read about the intonation patterns of question tags. Play the tape and ask them to write R if the intonation rises at the end (a real question) and F if it falls (expecting agreement).

Answers
1 F 2 R 3 F 4 F 5 F 6 R

SPEAKING AND WRITING

1 **Aim: to practise using question tags; to practise speaking.**

● Ask the students to go round the class giving their opinions about music and following it up with their two or three ideas to continue the conversation. Encourage students to use question tags where possible and to respond with opinions of their own. Each student should have short conversations with at least two other students.

2 **Aim: to practise writing a short report; to practise using the linking words *on the whole, in my opinion, the trouble is, in fact.***

● Lead a class discussion on music for a few minutes. Encourage everyone to give an opinion. Include the linking words as much as possible to show how they are used.

● Ask the students to write a report on the class's opinion about music.
You may like to ask them to do this activity for homework.

Progress check 1–5

GENERAL COMMENTS

You can work through this Progress check in the order shown, or concentrate on areas which may have caused difficulty in Lessons 1 to 5. You can also let the students choose the activities they would like to or feel the need to do.

VOCABULARY

1 Aim: to present adjectives of nationality and nouns for the people from different countries.

● The students may have already learnt the words used to describe people from and the nationality of their own country and its immediate neighbours. They may not have learnt the rules on how to form these adjectives and nouns. You may need to spend some time checking that they can form the nationality word, which may be fairly different from the country word (*Denmark, Danish, Norway, Norwegian*). Then ask them to form the word for the people. Ask them to complete the chart.

● You can continue to practise this vocabulary with other nationalities and people, and you may like to check the students know what language or languages are spoken there as well.

Answers

country	nationality	people
Germany	German	the Germans
Hungary	Hungarian	the Hungarians
India	Indian	the Indians
Japan	Japanese	the Japanese

2 Aim: to present some techniques for dealing with difficult words.

● The more competent students will already be using these different techniques. Encourage students to adopt these techniques for all new items of vocabulary, before looking a word up in the dictionary.

3 Aim: to explain the purpose of the *Wordbank*.

● It is important that the students realise that language acquisition in general and vocabulary acquisition in particular is only effective if they take an active part in the process. This means choosing words which are personally useful and recording them. Most students will only be able to retain about eight or nine words a lesson, so while the twenty or so words presented in the box are the most important ones to learn, the students must make the final selection. The *Wordbank* is designed to help the students organise their vocabulary records in a systematic way.

GRAMMAR

1 Aim: to revise asking for help in the classroom.

Answers
1 How do you spell Italian?
2 What's the English for *heureux?*
3 How do you pronounce A-M-E-R-I-C-A-N?
4 What does impatient mean?
5 What does *repeat* mean?

2 Aim: to revise adverbs and adverbial phrases of frequency; to present an opportunity for reflection on the students' learning habits.

● Make sure the students answer the questions according to their own learning habits.

3 Aim: to revise the difference between the present simple and the present continuous.

Answers
We're **going** to Italy next week. We're **taking** the plane. Usually we **have** two weeks' holiday, but this year we're **having** four. We **aren't taking** the car because the journey **takes** too long. We're **staying** at a friend's house in Varese. Usually he **works** in Milan, but at the moment he's **spending** the summer in New York.

4 Aim: to revise *after* + *-ing*.

Answers
1 **After** getting dressed, I have breakfast.
2 **After** having a cup of coffee, I start work.
3 **After** saying hello to my friends, I go and see my boss.
4 **After** opening my mail, I make some phone calls.
5 **After** checking my appointments for the next day, I leave the office at 5pm.
6 **After** having a drink with friends, I go home.

5 Aim: to revise *before + -ing.*

Answers
1 **Before** having breakfast, I get dressed.
2 **Before** starting work, I have a cup of coffee.
3 **Before** going to see my boss, I say hello to my friends.
4 **Before** making some phone calls, I open my mail.
5 **Before** leaving the office at 5pm, I check my appointments for the next day.
6 **Before** going home, I have a drink with friends.

6 Aim: to revise adjectives ending in *-ed* and *-ing.*

Answers
1 disappointing 2 boring 3 annoyed 4 frightening
5 excited 6 delighted

7 Aim: to revise question tags.

Answers
1 isn't she? 2 don't you? 3 does she?
4 haven't you? 5 are they? 6 doesn't he?

SOUNDS

1 Aim: to focus on stress change in words for countries and nationalities.
● ▭ Explain that the stressed syllable in the word for a nationality is not always the same as it is in the word for the country. Ask the students to listen and tick the words where the stress changes.

Answers
3 Canada   Canadian
4 Japan   Japanese
5 Italy   Italian

2 Aim: to focus on the sounds /ɪ/ and /iː/.
● Many learners, especially speakers of Latin-based languages, have problems with these sounds because there is no differentiation in their own language.

● Write the words on the board and underline the vowel sounds. Spend a few minutes with the class asking them to repeat these minimal pairs.

Answers
/ɪ/: hit bit sit bin sin gin bid hid
/iː/: heat beat seat bean seen Jean bead heed

● ▭ Play the tape and continue to give them practise in distinguishing between the two sounds.

3 Aim: to focus on the attitude of speakers.
● Ask your students if they think English sounds softer or harsher than their own language. Explain that in English, even if the speakers are angry or passionate

about something, they don't always show this in their voice.
● Check that everyone understands what the adjectives mean. If necessary, describe their meaning by saying something in the manner of the adjective.

● ▭ Play the tape and ask them to decide which adjective can be used to describe how the speakers sound. Explain that they don't have to understand every word.

Answers
1 excited
2 angry
3 impatient

● You may like to ask the students to turn to page 115 and read the tapescript to check how much they understood. Don't spend too much time explaining the meaning of difficult words as this is not the aim of the activity.

● Ask if the students think their language sounds similar to English.

SPEAKING AND WRITING

1 Aim: to practise speaking; to practise using the present continuous.
● Ask the students to work in pairs. Make sure they all know who is Student A and who is Student B. Explain that Student B must guess what is happening in Student A's photo. Student A only has to answer the questions with *yes* or *no.*

● You may like to continue this activity with photos or pictures of your own.

2 Aim: to understand text organisation; to prepare for the writing practice in activity 4.
● Ask the students to work alone and to put the sentences in order.

● Ask the students to work in pairs and to check their answers.

Answers
a f g c i d b e h

3 Aim: to practise writing about a sequence of actions; to practise using *before* and *after* clauses.
● Ask the students to join the sentences in activity 2 using suitable *before* and *after* clauses.

4 Aim: to practise writing about a sequence of actions; to compare traditional celebrations in different countries.
● Ask the students to write a paragraph describing how they spend New Year's Eve in their country. Suggest that they use the paragraph they wrote in activity 3 as a model. You may like to ask the students to do this activity for homework.

6
GENERAL COMMENTS

Vocabulary

In the vocabulary box are the words which are generated by the lesson material and which are considered to be suitable for the learner to focus on at this stage of the course. There will be other words which may be new, but it is important for the students to realise that it is more helpful to be selective about the vocabulary load. Many students will only be able to learn and retain ten or twelve new words from a lesson. The activities which accompany the vocabulary items are designed firstly to help the students explore the meaning, and secondly, to encourage the organisation of the new words according to personal categories.

Motivation

The reading and listening texts in *Reward* are selected to appeal to the interest of as many students as possible. There are many factors likely to contribute to or compromise the students' motivation, such as relevance to the learner's personal requirements, level of difficulty, layout and length. The text about how Josephine Wilson and Nguyen Van Tuan met was chosen for its broad, multi-national appeal. Above all, the task which accompanies it has been designed to provide an artificial motivation in its problem-solving nature, and to reduce the amount of reading each student has to do by *jigsawing* it, the technique used in Lesson 3, which gives part of a text to one student and another part of it to his or her partner. This involves an information gap between the two students and leads to a communicative exchange of information.

VOCABULARY AND SPEAKING

1 Aim: to present the vocabulary in the box; to talk about personal qualities in friends.

● Ask the students to work in pairs and to think about someone they like. Ask them to tick the words to describe their friend's qualities.

● Encourage the students to suggest other qualities they like their friends to have. Make sure you revise as much vocabulary to do with personal characteristics as possible.

2 Aim: to practise using the vocabulary in the box; to focus on adjectives formed from nouns.

● Encourage the students to extend their vocabulary by forming adjectives from the nouns in the box. Suggest that they do this as often as they can with new vocabulary. You may like to write on the board a chart like the one below for them to copy into their vocabulary books.

noun	*verb*	*adjective*
attraction	attract	attractive

Answers

intelligent, sincere, reliable, good looking, kind, honest, patient, single-minded, serious, ideal, optimistic, open, talented, confident, ambitious, informal, faithful

3 Aim: to practise talking about when you and your students first met.

● Ask the students where they met each other. Did any of them know each other before they came to the class? Did they all meet on the same day?

● Ask some supplementary questions such as what time it was, what day it was, what you were wearing, what the weather was like etc.

READING

1 Aim: to prepare for reading.

● Ask the students to read the introduction and to find out who Josephine Wilson and Nguyen Van Tuan are. Ask if anyone can predict which of the words in the vocabulary box will be used to describe them.

2 Aim: to prepare for reading; to predict the answers for check questions; to practise writing.

● Explain that thinking about answers to the questions is a way of helping the students to predict what the text might be about. They can do this activity together. It can be done orally around the class if you don't have much time, but it works better if they write full answers.

3 Aim: to read for specific information; to complete the answers they wrote in activity 2.

● Explain to the students that each one is going to read part of a passage and is going to describe what they have read to their partner. Ask them to turn to the relevant Communication activities at the back of the book, read their passage and then return to Lesson 6, page 15.

4 Aim: to check reading comprehension; to help the students fill in missing information about each other's texts.

● Explain again that each student in each pair has read a text either about Josephine Wilson or about Nguyen Van Tuan. Ask them to work together and answer all the questions in activity 2.

Answers
1 She was doing some shopping.
2 He was living with Cathy Kelly.
3 He was feeling lonely and suffering from culture shock.
4 They were attending Cathy Kelly's party.
5 He was still learning English.
6 She bought him some clothes.
7 She trained to be an actress.
8 She took him to concerts, political meetings and the theatre.
9 He was coping very well.
10 They were seeing each other every day.

GRAMMAR

1 Aim: to focus on the form of the past simple and the past continuous.

● Ask the students to read the information in the grammar box.

● Ask if anyone can spot examples of the past simple and the past continuous in the texts, both in the introduction and in the texts themselves. Write these on the board.

● Ask the students to read their text again, and underline the verbs in the past simple and past continuous. They should write down the irregular past simple verbs. For extra practice you could ask them to read their partner's text as well.

Answers
Irregular verbs: came, met, was, spoke, saw, knew, took, told

2 Aim: to focus on the distinction between the past simple and the past continuous.

● Ask the students to read the sentences and to choose the best tense. You can do this activity orally with the whole class.

Answers
1 He **was working** in a store, when she **came** in.
2 She **was doing** the shopping, when he first **saw** her.
3 While he **was living** with Cathy Kelly, he **met** Josephine.
4 Cathy Kelly **was having** a party when she **introduced** Nguyen to her.

LISTENING AND WRITING

1 Aim: to prepare for listening.

● Explain that the listening text contains a description of two people talking about how they first met. The students should look at the phrases, which come from the text, and use them to predict the answers to the questions. Do this activity orally with the whole class.

2 Aim: to practise listening for specific information.

● 🔊 Play the tape and ask the students to listen and find the answers to the questions.

Answers
1 At an end-of-term party.
2 Just before last Christmas.
3 He was standing around with no one to talk to. She was talking to some friends.
4 He has a great sense of humour and they both have similar interests and taste in music.

3 Aim: to check listening comprehension.

● Ask the students to work together and to check their answers.

● 🔊 Play the tape again.

4 Aim: to prepare for writing; to practise using the words in the vocabulary box and the structures in the grammar box.

● Ask the students to think of the friend they thought of in *Vocabulary and speaking* activity 1. They should think of answers to the questions.

5 Aim: to prepare for writing.

● Ask the students to go round the class finding out about each other's friends. Encourage them to write notes.

6 Aim: to practise writing.

● Ask the students to write a paragraph either about their own special friend or one of their colleague's friends. Tell students to use their notes and the answers to the questions in activity 4 to help them.

● You may like to ask the students to do this activity for homework.

7

GENERAL COMMENTS

Collocations

One of the most effective ways of developing the intermediate student's vocabulary and ability to speak fluent, confident sounding English is to explore collocations. A single noun on its own may convey the meaning of what the student wants to say or write, but a suitable adjective which goes with the noun will give the impression of greater fluency. In this lesson, there are some activities for collocating adjectives with nouns and verbs with nouns. However, you may find it useful to do this type of activity every time there is a presentation of new vocabulary.

Lesson plan

Each textbook lesson of *Reward* corresponds to a classroom lesson of about 60 minutes. Some lessons will take more or less time, but they are all designed to be a careful balance of a warm-up activity to introduce the theme, the vocabulary and/or grammar focus introduced by reading and or listening practice, backed up by an explanation of the target structure and exercises, and rounded off by some sounds work, writing or speaking. The plan of the textbook lesson corresponds loosely to the ideal classroom lesson plan. Each syllabus in the course design is linked communicatively to the theme of the lesson, so every activity will have some communicative context. If you have more time, or need further practice, the Resource Pack activities will contribute 20 or 30 minutes extra work.

VOCABULARY AND READING

1 Aim: to present the words in the vocabulary box; to focus on verbs and nouns which go together.

● Ask the students to close their eyes and to think about their childhood memories of holidays. Ask them to think of words which they associate with these memories.

● Ask the students to say the words they've thought of. Write them on the board. Are all the words very similar or very different?

● Do some work on collocation by asking the students to underline the verbs and then look at the words in the box and put the verbs with the nouns. There may be several possibilities.

● If you have time, you may like to ask the students to think of other verbs which go with the nouns and other nouns which go with the verbs.

● Explain that these are some important words from the passage they are going to read.

Answers
buy tickets, carry bags, complain about cost, family, neighbours, cost money, invest in tickets, memories, invite family, neighbours, play games, spend money, waste money, write programmes

2 Aim: to practise reading for specific information.

● Ask the students to read *Investing in memories* and to tick the things which made the day trips to the seaside so memorable.

Answers
careful preparation: the special programme sent in advance
organised games and competitions: football matches, treasure hunts
prizes for winners: usually an old sporting cup from a junk shop
lots of people: he invited family, neighbours and children
driving along in the car: the games they used to play

3 Aim: to focus on techniques to deal with difficult words.

● This activity gives the students some useful help in working out the meaning of some words which may be unfamiliar. The help is not designed to give the exact meaning of the word, but only the general idea. On many occasions, this will be all the students will need to get the main idea of the passage. It's important for them to realise that they will be more effective in their reading if they avoid looking for the exact meaning of every single word.

4 Aim: to practise speaking; to check reading comprehension.

● Encourage the students to give their reactions to the text by talking about the writer's uncle. Do they know of anyone as memorable as this?

GRAMMAR

1 Aim: to focus on affirmative and negative forms of *used to*.

● Ask the students to read the information in the grammar box and then do the exercises.

● Make it clear to the students that these are all false statements. You may like to do this activity in writing, as it may make *Sounds* activity 2 easier if they have a script.

Answers

1 He didn't use to have a beard.
  He had a moustache.
2 He didn't use to smoke cigars.
  He used to smoke cigarettes.
3 They didn't use to have boring trips.
  They used to have wonderful trips.
4 They didn't use to go to the mountains.
  They used to go to the sea.
5 He didn't use to invite only the family.
  He used to invite neighbours and their children as well.
6 The fun didn't use to start when they arrived.
  It used to start as soon as they left home.

---

2 Aim: to focus on the difference between *used to* and *would*.

● Explain that sometimes you can use both *used to* and *would*, and sometimes you can only use *used to*. Remind students that *would* is only used to talk about typical behaviour or a past habit. Ask them to tick the sentences where you can use both.

Answers

As a child, I **used to** spend my holidays in the mountains. We **used to** have a chalet near Geneva. We **used to/would** go there for about a month in the summer, when it **used to** be sunny and for Christmas, when there **used to/would** be lots of snow.

SOUNDS

Aim: to focus on contrastive stress.

● Make sure the students realise that this activity makes use of their answers to *Grammar* activity 1.

● 🖭 Play the tape. Ask the students to listen to the stress and intonation when you correct someone.

● Now ask the students to repeat the sentences. You can do this orally with the whole class.

SPEAKING AND WRITING

1 Aim: to practise speaking; to prepare for writing.
● Ask the students to work in groups of two or three and to talk about the way things used to be in the past. They should use the prompts to help them.

2 Aim: to practise writing a description of life in the past.
● Ask the students to think about their holidays in the past and to use the linking words *when, after a while, eventually, now,* to write a description of life in the past.

● You may like to ask the students to do this activity for homework.

8

GENERAL COMMENTS

Using the tapescripts

The listening comprehension passage in this lesson is rather long and you may find it helpful to use the tapescript at some point. The tapescripts are included primarily for reference purposes; there may be occasions when you or the students need to check what exactly has been said. It is not a good idea for students to follow them while they are listening to the tape, at least during the first listening, because this may encourage them to think that they have to understand every single word in order to understand the general sense. In real-life situations, the students will be constantly confronted by language which is more complex than their present level would allow them to cope with. This situation is simulated in the classroom, so that the students can better prepare themselves for language use in real life. The tasks which accompany the listening material are nevertheless graded to suit the intermediate students' level of competence, and can be performed even if the passage is quite difficult. However, at some stage, perhaps between the first and the second listening, you may want to allow the students to read the tapescript. Make it clear that this is an exception not the rule. If you use the tapescripts too often, the listening material may become easier, but you may not be providing the right kind of overall training in listening comprehension.

VOCABULARY AND LISTENING

1 Aim: to present the theme of the lesson.

● Draw on the board a smiling face and a sad face. Ask the students to suggest things or situations which make them happy or sad. Write their answers on the board.

● The theme of the lesson is contained in the title. Explain that the students are going to hear a woman describe an occasion when she was cold, lost, hungry and alone during a trip to Russia. Write on the board *cold, lost, hungry, alone*. Ask the students if they have ever been, or felt any of these things. Do this activity orally, with the whole class.

2 Aim: to present the vocabulary in the box; to pre-teach some important words; to prepare for listening.

● Some students may not know the meaning of some of these words. Few of them have been presented before, so you may want to spend some time exploring their meaning.

● This categorisation activity also encourages the students to prepare for listening. Ask them to predict which words in the box are likely to go with *cold, lost, hungry* and *alone*.

● Encourage the students to add words they used in activity 1 to their categories.

3 Aim: to listen for main ideas.

● ▣ The students should now be well-prepared for listening, so play the tape and ask them to tick the word which describes her state.

Answer
She was alone.

4 Aim: to present the target structure; to prepare for *Grammar* activity 1; to provide an opportunity for a second listening.

● Explain that the sentences describe events which happen one after another. Ask the students to number the events in the order they happen.

Answers
1 She forgot to ring her friend
2 She was leaving London.
3 She was walking out into the hall.
4 A crowd of people surrounded her.
5 Her German friend disappeared.
6 She felt lonely and rather foolish.
7 She was starting to panic.
8 Someone tapped her on the shoulder.
9 She called Sergei.
10 He was out.
11 She was getting out of the car.
12 Three soldiers stopped her.
13 They heard her speaking English.
14 They let her through.
15 She had to wait at reception.
16 The theatre in St Petersburg sent a fax.

● ▣ Play the tape again and check the students' answers.

5 Aim: to listen for main ideas.

● ▣ Refer the students back to the statements mentioned in activity 3. Ask them to listen to the next part and decide how she felt.

Answer
She was cold and lost.

6 Aim: to focus on *as, when, while, as soon as* and *until*.

● Ask the students to discuss if the statements are true or false. The statements that are false are grammatically incorrect.

Answers
1 True   2 True   3 False   4 False   5 True   6 False

GRAMMAR

1 Aim: to focus on the link words *when, as soon as, as, while, just as, until.*

● Ask the students to read the information in the grammar box and then do the exercises.

● Ask the students to use the linking words to join the two parts of the sentences in activity 4.

● When you correct this activity, there may be more than one possible answer, so discuss alternative answers with the students.

Possible answers

1 She forgot to ring Sergei **until** she was leaving London.
2 **As** she walked out of the hall, a crowd of people surrounded her.
3 **As soon as** her German friend disappeared, she felt lonely and rather foolish.
4 She was starting to panic **when** someone tapped her on the shoulder.
5 **When** she called Sergei, he was out.
6 **When** she got out of the car, three soldiers stopped her.
7 **As soon as** they heard her speaking English, they let her through.
8 She had to wait at reception **until** the theatre in St Petersburg sent a fax.

2 Aim: to practise using the past simple and the past continuous.

● Ask the students to correct the statements from part 2 in *Vocabulary and listening* activity 6.

Answers

3 She was enjoying the walk **when** she got lost.
4 She was standing by the side of the road **when** a car stopped.
6 **When** the driver said 'taxi', she was very relieved.

READING AND WRITING

1 Aim: to practise writing; to prepare for reading.

● Ask the students to predict part 3 of the story by trying to answer the questions. Make sure they understand that they cannot answer these questions completely, but they can answer most of each one by simply using the words to write affirmative statements and leaving a blank if they cannot guess anything.

● Write up a few of the affirmative statements below so they get the idea.

Possible answers

1 Next, she went to _____.
2 _____ was waiting for her at the station.
3 The director didn't recognise her because ____ .
4 She got to the theatre by ____.
5 ____ invited her to stay.
6 Natasha lived in ____.
7 ____ was sharing her flat.
8 Natasha couldn't afford to feed Claudia because ____.
9 Claudia bought ____ on the streets.

● The most significant difficulty with this activity will be the position of the different clauses within the sentences. It may be easier to do the activity orally and with the whole class.

2 Aim: to read for specific information.

● In activity 1, the students have prepared their own reading comprehension check. Ask them to turn to Communication activity 6 on page 99, and read the last part and fill in any information they had left out or correct anything which is wrong.

● Leave plenty of time to correct this activity.

3 Aim: to practise writing paragraphs.

● Ask the students to follow the instructions and to write about Claudia's experiences when she was alone and cold, lost, and hungry. The preparation in *Grammar* activities 1 and 2 and *Writing and listening* activities 3 and 4 should allow them to do this activity fairly easily.

● You may like to ask the students to do this activity for homework.

9

GENERAL COMMENTS

Non-defining relative clauses

The students will have seen on many occasions examples of non-defining relative clauses, although this is the first time they have been presented as a target structure for a lesson in *Reward*. The most important aspect to note and to draw to their attention is that the non-defining relative clause is separated from the rest of the sentence by a comma. The defining relative clause has no comma, and is more common in written than in spoken English because it is quite formal. Unlike a defining relative clause, you cannot replace a non-defining relative clause with *that*.

Reading text types

It is to be hoped that the students will respond positively to *Chocolate – like falling in love,* not just because the topic may appeal to them, but because the text is easy to read. In real life we don't just read long passages of language, but short snippets as well. If this passage had been laid out so that it was in one single paragraph, it would be much more indigestible and would risk compromising the students' motivation. In *Reward*, a broad variety of text types is used to practise reading comprehension, with both short and long passages.

READING AND VOCABULARY

1 Aim: to present the topic of the lesson.
● Find out how many of your students like chocolate. Ask them how often and when they eat it, and what kind they like. Is there anyone who also enjoys the drink?

● Find out how much chocolate is eaten by your class in a week. You may want to collect this information anonymously for fear of shaming the more indulgent!

2 Aim: to present the words in the vocabulary box; to prepare for reading.
● Explain the meaning of these words by asking students to decide which words they would associate with chocolate. To do this, you may have to use other word associations to explain the meaning.

● Encourage the students to think of other words which they associate with chocolate.

3 Aim: to practise reading for main ideas.
● Ask the students why chocolate might be like falling in love.

● Ask the students to read the passage and find out why it's called *Chocolate – like falling in love.*

> **Answer**
> It contains small amounts of a chemical which is naturally present in the brain, especially when we fall in love.

4 Aim: to help comprehension; to read for main ideas.
● Ask the students to read the passage again and to match the paragraphs with the headings.

> **Answers**
> **history:** 1, 2, 3, 4, 5, 6, 7,
> **present day facts:** 8, 9, 10, 11, 12, 13
> **interesting incidents:** 14, 15

5 Aim: to practise reading to understand text organisation; to focus on the target structure.
● This activity encourages the students to focus on the implicit and explicit organisation of the text, using examples of the non-defining relative clause. Explain that these clauses came from the original passage. The students should re-read it and decide where the clauses can go.

> **Answers**
> 1 Chocolate, **which people enjoy all over the world,** first came from Central America.
> 2 The Aztecs made a greasy, bitter drink called *Xocoatl,* **which means 'bitter water',** from cocoa beans...
> 3 The explorer Cortes, **who first tried chocolate in 1519,** was the first person to bring chocolate to Europe.
> 4 Henri Nestlé, **who was Peter's colleague,** developed the process.
> 5 The world's largest chocolate model, **which weighed nearly 200 kg,** was a 10 m by 5 m representation of the Olympic Centre in Barcelona.
> 6 The world's largest chocolate model, which weighed nearly 200 kg, was a 10 m by 5 m representation of the Olympic Centre in Barcelona, **where they held the Olympic Games in 1992.**

GRAMMAR

1 Aim: to focus on non-defining relative clauses.

● Ask the students to read the information in the grammar box and then do the exercises.

● The passage was chosen for its high number of non-defining relative clauses. Ask students to read it again and to note down all the examples of this structure.

● Check that the students have done this successfully orally with the whole class.

Answers

According to H H Bancroft, **who was a historian**
Coenrad van Houten, **who was Dutch** …
Joseph Fry, **who lived in England** …
Daniel Peter, **who was a confectioner** …
Women, **who buy more than two-thirds** …
…except the Scots, who eat 30 per cent more.
the chemical phenylethylamine, **which is also naturally present** …

2 Aim: to focus on the difference between *who*, *which* and *where* in non-defining relative clauses.

● Ask the students to complete the sentences with *who*, *which* or *where*.

Answers

1 which 2 who 3 which 4 who
5 which 6 which 7 where 8 where

3 Aim: to focus on the clause which contains the extra information.

● You may need to explain that in two pieces of information, you will have to decide which is the *base* information and which is the *extra* information. In classroom exercises there is often no right or wrong answer about this, although in real life, the context will usually make this clear.

Answers

1 Champagne, **which** is one of the most expensive drinks in the world, comes from France.
2 The Brazilians, **who** export the most coffee in the world, produce a million tonnes a year.
3 Dr John Pemberton, **who** invented Coca Cola, lived in Atlanta USA.
4 The avocado pear, **which** contains the most calories of any fruit, has more protein than milk.
5 The Incas, **who** lived in South America in the fifteenth century, discovered popcorn.
6 The durian fruit, **which** has a disgusting taste and smell, is considered by some people to be a delicacy.

● You may like to discuss the difference in meaning if you rewrite the sentences above changing the base and the extra information.

SPEAKING AND WRITING

1 Aim: to practise using non-defining relative clauses.

● Ask the students to work in pairs and to make a list of three well-known things, people or places. You may like to ask for some suggestions and write them on the board.

2 Aim: to practise using non-defining relative clauses; to practise speaking.

● Ask the students to join another pair of students and find out how much extra information can be added to the list in 1.

● Decide which is the most important information, and which is the extra information.

3 Aim: to practise writing sentences; to practise using the non-defining relative clause.

● Ask the students to write sentences combining the base and extra information with non-defining relative clauses.

● You may like to ask the students to do this activity for homework.

10

GENERAL COMMENTS

Cross-cultural awareness

This lesson continues the training in cross-cultural awareness by presenting the students with material which describes a series of situations in which *gaffes* occurred. It is important to stress to the students that the training is not designed to make them so sensitive about their behaviour that they become too nervous to do anything. It is, however, intended to challenge cultural assumptions and to make them aware that they may not always be able to transfer what they consider to be acceptable behaviour into other cultural contexts. The material, in the form of problem-page type letters focuses on several important social conventions and rituals: gestures, leave-taking, invitations, gift-giving, degrees of formality and behaviour in public places.

Verbs with two objects

The students will have seen many examples of verbs with two objects, but this is the first time they have been presented as a target structure in *Reward*. You may want to add to the information in the grammar box; for example, *explain* and *suggest* can take two objects, but there needs to be the preposition *to* before the indirect object, for example, *Explain to your students the meaning of the new vocabulary and suggest some practice exercises to them.*

READING AND VOCABULARY

1 Aim: to practise reading for main ideas.

● Ask the students if they have ever been in a situation in which a mistake or a misunderstanding has arisen. Was the situation with people from their own culture or from a foreign one?

● Ask the students to read the letters, and try to decide what the mistake or misunderstanding was.

2 Aim: to check comprehension; to compare customs and behaviour in different cultures; to practise speaking.

● Ask the students to work in pairs and to check their answers to activity 1.

● An explanation for each situation will be given in the listening passage.

3 Aim: to present the vocabulary in the box.

● Ask the students to look at the words in the vocabulary box decide what part of speech they are. Encourage other students to explain any difficult words. Many of these words may be new, so this activity of matching words and their definitions is designed to help students with unfamiliar vocabulary items.

> **Answers**
> 1 meal 2 customer 3 crowded 4 bunch
> 5 colleague 6 casual 7 wallet 8 waiter 9 mean
> 10 hurt 11 cross 12 present

LISTENING

1 Aim: to practise listening for specific information.

● ⌨ The students should be well-prepared for this listening activity by the reading and discussion activity which has preceded it. Explain that they are going to hear an expert on cross-cultural behaviour explaining what the mistakes or misunderstandings were.

> **Answer**
> The English hostess thought Lu wanted to leave very quickly. In China the evening finishes when the last dish is served.
> Red roses are a symbol of intimacy and an uneven number is more appropriate.
> In Britain it's common to pay for your own share of a restaurant bill.
> In Britain it's usual for people to give up their seats in buses to elderly people.
> A stranger being warm and friendly is not necessarily a sign of true friendship and it takes time to get to know someone well.

2 Aim: to check comprehension; to provide an opportunity for a second listening.

● In pairs, ask the students to discuss, in as much detail as possible, the explanations for the misunderstandings.

GRAMMAR AND FUNCTIONS

1 Aim: to focus on verbs which take two objects.
- Ask the students to read the information in the grammar box and then to do the exercises.

- Encourage the students to find for themselves verbs which take two objects. This kind of inductive approach will help consolidate the learning of the structure.

> **Answers**
> invite, bring, take, give, offer, tell, show

2 Aim: to focus on verbs with two objects without using to and for.
- Explain that *to* is more often used when there is a sense of motion, and *for* is more symbolic. For example,
I took a bottle of wine to the host.
= I went to the host and handed him a bottle of wine.
I took a bottle of wine for the host.
= The bottle of wine was meant as a present for the host.

> **Answers**
> 1 She took her friends some flowers.
> 2 Can you give her the keys?
> 3 I'm bringing you a nice cake.
> 4 Could you send them a cheque?
> 5 They'll order you a taxi at reception.
> 6 Write them a postcard when you get there.

3 Aim: to focus on apologising and complaining.
- You may like to do this activity orally with the whole class. Point out that there may be more than one possible answer.

> **Possible answers**
> 1 Would you mind not smoking so much?
> 2 Could you lend me some money?
> 3 Could you turn the television down?
> 4 Would you mind not driving so fast?
> 5 I'm sorry, but my watch isn't working.
> 6 I'm sorry I'm late.

- Ask the students to think of suitable responses to these sentences.

SOUNDS

Aim: to focus on intonation used in apologies and complaints.
- You may like to mention that British people try to be as polite as possible when they complain, and that they often use the language of apologising to do so. The main difference can be heard in the intonation, with the complaint sounding more forceful.

- ▭ Ask the students to listen to the two intonation patterns. In the first sentence the speaker is complaining and in the second sentence, apologising.

- Ask the students to work in pairs and to repeat each sentence either as an apology or a complaint. The other student should try to say which is which.

- You may want to point out that it isn't necessary for them to imitate the British when they apologise or complain, but they may need to recognise the difference between the two when they hear an ambiguous sentence.

SPEAKING

1 Aim: to practise speaking; to help the students be aware that behaviour can vary according to individuals as well as cultures.
- This activity explores the differences that occur among people who come from either the same culture or different cultures. Ask the students to go through the list and discuss what they would do if there was a misunderstanding or they have made a mistake.

2 Aim: to practise speaking.
- Ask the students to work in groups of three or four and discuss situations where there was a misunderstanding or mistake. Do these kinds of misunderstanding and mistakes only occur with non-native speakers or can they occur with people from their own culture?

Progress check 6–10

GENERAL COMMENTS

You can work through this Progress check in the order shown, or concentrate on areas which may have caused difficulty in Lessons 6 to 10. You can also let the students choose the activities they would like to or feel the need to do.

VOCABULARY

1 Aim: to present strong adjectives.

● It's useful for the students to be aware of strong adjectives, as their use contributes greatly to the impression of fluency. Ask them if adjectives have strong forms in their own language. Can they think of other ways of intensifying adjectives?

> **Answers**
> annoying – infuriating, angry – furious,
> cold – freezing, frightening – terrifying,
> funny – hilarious, interesting – fascinating,
> pleased – delighted, silly – ridiculous,
> surprised – astonished

2 Aim: to focus on adjective prefixes.

● Explain that these prefixes can be added to many adjectives to give them the opposite meaning. Ask the students to give you an example of something *interesting* and something *uninteresting*, something *possible* and something *impossible*.

● Ask the students to write the opposite of the adjectives by adding a suitable prefix. You can do this activity orally with the whole class.

> **Answers**
> uncertain, unclear, impatient, incorrect, unfriendly,
> unkind, incomplete, unhappy, unimportant,
> immodest, imperfect

3 Aim: to focus on homophones.

● Explain that the spelling system of English is made more complicated by a number of words which have the same sound but different spelling. Ask the students if this occurs in their own language.

● Point out that the answers to this activity can be found in the vocabulary boxes in Lessons 6 to 10. This will therefore be a good opportunity to review the recent vocabulary.

> **Answers**
> bean – been, by – buy, beech – beach, bred – bread,
> plane – plain, waist – waste, right – write,

4 Aim: to help the students organise their vocabulary learning.

● Remind the students that they need to go back over their *Wordbanks* every so often. It also may be helpful to organise the words in different categories.

GRAMMAR

1 Aim: to revise the difference between the past simple and continuous.

> **Answers**
> An American who **was visiting** Russia, **wanted** to go on a wild bear hunt and **paid** a lot of money for the sport. The travel agent **took** the American to Moscow's Perdelino Forest. Suddenly, he **saw** a bear, and **decided** to get closer because he **hoped** to shoot it. A postman, who **was riding** past on his bicycle, **fell** off in surprise when he **spotted** the bear. The bear **came** over to the bicycle, **picked** it up and **rode** off. In fact, it wasn't a wild bear at all. It **was performing** at the local circus. The bear **escaped**, the postman **lost** his bicycle and the American **asked** for his money back.

2 Aim: to revise the difference between *used to* and *would*.

> **Answers**
> Howard Hughes, the American film producer, **lived** for fifteen years completely on his own. He **used to spend** all day lying on his bed watching films. He **would/used to** hate touching anything that **wasn't** sterile. He **used to** live on tinned chicken soup for weeks, and then **used to** change to a diet of ice cream. When he **died** he **was** a billionaire.

3 Aim: to revise the link words *just as, when, while, as soon as* and *until*.

> **Possible answers**
> 1 **As soon as** the traffic stopped, we ran across the road.
> 2 He stayed in bed **until** he got better.
> 3 **While** I was living in London, I spent a lot of time in the museums.
> 4 **When** I saw her, I waved to her.
> 5 **Just as** I was leaving, the phone rang.
> 6 She waited by the door **while** someone opened it.

4 Aim: to revise the use of non-defining relative clauses.

> **Possible answers**
> 1 Venice, **which** is in the north of Italy, stands on 118 islands.
> 2 The London Underground, **which** has 400 km of tunnels, is the longest in the world.
> 3 A Dutchman, **who** bought Manhattan island in 1626, only paid about $24.
> 4 Barbara Cartland, **who** is the world's most popular writer, has sold about 400 million copies of her romantic novels.
> 5 The oldest city in the world is Jericho, **which** had a population of 3000 people in 7,800 BC.
> 6 Women, **who** live longer than men, have an average life of 77 years.

5 Aim: to revise the use of verbs with two objects.

> **Answers**
> 1 I gave her a present.
> 2 She brought me a bottle of wine.
> 3 He passed her the dish.
> 4 We sent her a postcard.
> 5 My father taught schoolchildren French.
> 6 I showed the police my passport.

SOUNDS

1 Aim: to focus on words which are linked in connected speech.
- It is important to stress that in connected speech words are linked, and that this is perfectly acceptable in both formal and informal situations. Ask the students to read the rules concerning linking in connected speech.

2 Aim: to focus on word linking.
- Ask the students to listen and mark the words in the extract from Lesson 7 which are linked.

> **Answers**
> My uncle had a moustache, a good job in the Civil Service and used to smoke forty cigarettes a day. But when he organised day trips for our family he used to behave like a boy. Today, seventy years later, we still talk about the wonderful trips to the sea we used to have as children, and which our uncle used to organise.

WRITING AND SPEAKING

1 Aim: to focus on word order.
- In most passages there will be some words which contribute to the overall style, but which can be left out without affecting the overall meaning. Ask the students to decide which words can be left out. Make it clear that they cannot leave out two or more words together thus cutting phrases and even whole sentences. This is a writing activity in the sense that an awareness of word order is important even before writing.

> **Answers**
> A close friend of my mother lives in the country in Yorkshire, and she ~~often~~ goes to the ~~beautiful~~ town of Harrogate to do her ~~weekly~~ shopping. After doing the shopping she usually has tea in a ~~small~~ tea shop. One afternoon she was looking forward to having tea and she went to her usual tea shop, but it was crowded with people from the antiques fair. The waitress was ~~rather~~ embarrassed that there was no room for a regular customer, but she offered her a place at a ~~small~~ table, sharing with a ~~middle-aged~~ man. The lady was disappointed but wanted a cup of tea ~~very much~~, so she agreed. The waitress showed her a table by the ~~front~~ window, where the man was sitting. The man smiled ~~politely~~ then returned to his ~~paperback~~ book. After a few minutes he got up and left.
> The lady was drinking her tea when she noticed that there was a slice of ~~fruit~~ cake on the man's plate. She looked around ~~carefully~~ but there was no sign of him. She was feeling ~~extremely~~ hungry and it seemed a ~~dreadful~~ shame to waste it, so she picked it up and ate it. Just as she was finishing the cake, the man reappeared and returned to the table.

2 Aim: to focus on word order.
- Make it clear that the example words are not necessary, but can fit into the passage.

- Ask the students to think of six more words which can go into the passage and write them on a piece of paper.

3 Aim: to focus on word order.
- Ask the students to work in pairs and to pass the words they have written in activity 2 to their partner. Each student should try to decide where his or her partner's words can go in the passage.

- You can check the answers orally with the whole class.

- You may like to ask the students to do this activity for homework.

4 Aim: to practise speaking.
- If there is time, you can ask students to work in small groups and to share embarrassing experiences if they can remember them, or dare to talk about them!

11

GENERAL COMMENTS

Present perfect simple

The presentation of the present perfect simple in this lesson should be revision for most students, although this is the first time it has appeared in *Reward* with *yet, already* and *still*. Unless the students have a tense with similar meanings in their own language, they will find it difficult to use it properly. Furthermore, American English usage is slightly different to that of British English, in that it uses the past simple on occasions when British English might use a present perfect. It may be one of those structures which are very difficult for you to teach, and for your students to learn, and in these circumstances, we can only hope to create the conditions for acquisition of the structure through regular exposure. It is important to remember that mistakes in usage of the present perfect rarely cause any problems of comprehensibility, and if, after this lesson, the students still have difficulties with it, it may be better to continue with the course rather than wait and make sure they get it right.

Questionnaires

Questionnaires are one of the most popular text types in real life. Most of us enjoy reading and answering them to find out more about ourselves. One possible reason for this is that they are among the rare text types which are naturally written in the second person. For these reasons, they make useful material for the communicative classroom.

READING

Aim: to introduce the topic of the lesson; to practise reading a questionnaire.

● This questionnaire is designed mainly to introduce the topic of the lesson, which is closely linked to the use of the target structure. It is important to convey the idea that the present perfect simple can be used to talk about things which have already been done or haven't yet been done, and the subject of the questionnaire focuses on the reader's potential for procrastination.

● Ask the students to read the questionnaire and to answer the questions.

● The students may like to work in pairs and talk about their answers, but they will also be asked to do this at the end of the lesson. Ask one or two students for their feedback at this stage, but not everyone.

● Point out that an explanatory score sheet can be found in Communication activity 14 on page 102.

LISTENING AND VOCABULARY

1 Aim: to prepare for listening.

● Explain that the tapescript contains some strange words or phrases. Ask the students to read it and look for anything they find strange.

● Check the students' answers. Can they suggest what should replace the strange words?

2 Aim: to practise listening for specific information; to prepare for the presentation of the target structure.

● 🎧 Play the tape and ask the students to underline anything which is different from what they hear.

Answers to activities 2 and 3

IAN Hi, Kate. How are you getting on?

KATE Hey, what are you doing here? I didn't expect you until later.

IAN Well, I've already finished everything I had to do at work, so I thought I'd come back and **help you.** I know you've had a **busy** day.

KATE I've had a extremely busy day, and it hasn't finished yet. Did you remember we've got Paul and Hannah for dinner tonight?

IAN Yes, I did. Have you got everything you need?

KATE Well, I've already done the shopping, but I haven't **bought** the wine yet.

IAN I'll do that. Have you **picked up** the children yet?

KATE No, I haven't done that yet. They're still at school.

IAN OK. Well, I'll get them when I buy the wine.

KATE No, they've got their sports club, so they'll be there until about six. You're more important here. Have you **collected** the car from the garage yet? It should be ready by now.

IAN No, I haven't. I'll go to the garage later. Now, what's next?

KATE Well, the kitchen is **clean,** but you could check the bathroom for me.

IAN OK. Have you **thrown away** the pile of newspapers in the front room?

KATE No, they're still **lying** on the table.

IAN I'll **take out** the rubbish as well.

KATE I've already done that. Now, I haven't started cooking yet, and it's getting late. When you've got the wine, can you **lay** the table? Here's the table cloth and knives and forks. And **mend** the television. It still doesn't work. And **wrap up** your mother's birthday present. It still needs wrapping paper. And **turn on** the heating. It's getting quite cold in here.

IAN Oh dear, it's one of those days.

● Ask the students to check their answers in pairs.

3 Aim: to present the vocabulary in the box.

● Check that everyone understands what the words in the vocabulary box mean.

● Ask the students to replace the words they have underlined with words from the vocabulary box.

> **Answers**
> See previous page

4 Aim: to focus on the target structure.

● Ask the students to remember the conversation they have heard and to put a tick by the things Kate has done and to put a cross by the things she hasn't done. The students can do this activity in pairs.

> **Answers**
> do the shopping ✓
> take out the rubbish ✓
> lay the table ✗
> buy the wine ✗
> collect the car ✗
> start cooking ✗
> clean the kitchen ✓
> throw away the newspapers ✗
> pick up the children ✗
> clean the bathroom ✗
> wrap up birthday presents ✗
> mend the television ✗
> turn on the heating ✗

5 Aim: to provide an opportunity for a second listening; to check the answers to activities 1, 2, 3 and 4.

● ▭ Play the tape again and ask the students to check their answers.

GRAMMAR

1 Aim: to practise using the present perfect simple with *yet* and *already*.

● Ask the students to read the information in the grammar box and then to do the exercises.

● This exercise allows the students to use the new structure and time expressions to describe what has happened in the conversation.

> **Answers**
> Kate has already done the shopping, taken out the rubbish and cleaned the kitchen. They haven't laid the table, bought the wine, collected the car, started cooking, thrown away the newspapers, picked up the children, cleaned the bathroom, wrapped up the birthday present, mended the television and turned on the heating. In fact, Ian hasn't done anything yet.

2 Aim: to focus on *already, yet* and *still*.

● Ask the students to complete the sentences with *already, yet* and *still*.

> **Answers**
> It's half past eight in the morning, and Jack should be at school by nine but he's **still** in bed. He's **already** had breakfast because he brought it back to bed. He hasn't packed his bags **yet**, and he is **still** trying to make up his mind what to wear. He's **already** been late for school three times this week.

SPEAKING

1 Aim: to practise speaking; to practise using the present perfect simple.

● Begin this activity by telling your students what you've done or haven't done yet today.

● Ask the students if they've done certain things, for example,
> *Have you had a cup of coffee yet?*
> *Have you done any work yet?*
> *Have you had anything to eat yet?*
> *Have you written to your family yet?*
> *Have you done your homework yet?*

Elicit *yes/no* answers.

● Ask the students to work in pairs and to talk about their answers to the questionnaire. Encourage them to talk about what they've done today or recently.

2 Aim: to practise speaking; to practise using the present perfect simple.

● Ask the students to think about how much time they usually spend doing the activities.

● Find out who spends the most and the least time doing the activities.

3 Aim: to practise speaking; to practise using the present perfect simple.

● Ask the students to talk about if they have spent as much time as usual on the activities in 2 this week.

12

GENERAL COMMENTS

Listening to the radio in English

It may be useful to point out to your students that learning English is not confined to the classroom, and that they can hear and read English in many situations outside the classroom. You may be in a town where English-language broadcasts are clear enough for them to be heard by the students. The language used may pose some difficulties, but with carefully prepared tasks, this can be overcome. The activity in this lesson is designed to allow the students to listen to a news broadcast and to extract some meaning from it, but without demanding comprehension of every single word. Remind them that the words they are likely to recognise will be proper names, international words, cognates, nationalities, geographical locations, jobs and sports. The chart in the lesson can be used on future occasions with different news broadcasts. If your students need details about the BBC World Service broadcasts, they should write to BBC, Bush House, Strand, London, WC2, UK. There is a magazine published called *London Calling* which lists all the programmes and times in different parts of the world.

VOCABULARY AND LISTENING

1 Aim: **to present the vocabulary in the box; to pre-teach some difficult words; to prepare for listening.**

● Ask the students to make a list of important events in the news at the moment. How much good news and bad news is there? Do they know of other events which are happening at the moment which are more important, but aren't in the news?

● Ask the students to work in groups of two or three and to look at the words in the box. Ask them to explain to each other any words they don't understand or to look them up in the dictionary.

● Explain that not all the words are required for a full understanding of the news they will hear, but are useful words for this particular level. There is no need to expect that they will learn all of them.

● When the students have understood the words, ask them to categorise them according to the type of news they could be used to describe. Some words can go in more than one category. Not all the categories will necessarily be used.

Possible answers
Business and economics: currency, prices
Crime: bullet, bomb, gun, hijack, hostage, kidnap, terrorist
Disaster: gun, fire, gale
Famous people: president, prime minister, soldier
Government: defeat, election, left wing, lose, party, president, prime minister, right wing, win, victory

Law: judge, jury, lawyer
Leisure interests: club, match, party, stadium
Military: airforce, army, attack, battle, bomb, gun, navy, missile, officer, solider, win, war, troops, victory, weapon
Politics: defeat, demonstration, election, left wing, lose, party, president, prime minister, right wing, win, victory
Sport: club, match, party, team, player, stadium
Weather: lightning, rain, thunderstorm

2 Aim: **to practise listening for main ideas; to provide examples of the present perfect continuous.**

● Explain that the students will not necessarily understand everything in the news bulletin they are going to hear, but that they should be able to understand the main ideas. To do the activity, the students must understand the language of the task, so take time to check that everyone understands the words in the chart.

● 📼 Play the tape and ask the students to tick the news type they hear in each item. Some stories may be more than one type of news item.

Possible answers	1	2	3	4	5	6
Arts and culture						
Business and economics						
Crime	✓					
Disaster					✓	
Famous people						
Foreign Affairs		✓				
Government				✓		
Law						
Leisure interests						
Military						
Politics	✓					
Religion						
Social affairs		✓				
Sport			✓			
Traffic and transport				✓		
Weather						✓

3 Aim: **to review the words in the vocabulary box; to check comprehension; to provide an opportunity for a second listening.**

● This stage helps the students focus on the details of what they heard. Ask them to describe each news item in as much detail as possible. Check comprehension of the new items with the whole class.

● 📼 Play the tape again and ask the students to listen and check.

● Tell the students that the chart can be used on future occasions with other news bulletins, especially when they're listening to the news outside the classroom.

GRAMMAR

1 Aim: to practise forming the present perfect continuous.

● Ask the students to read the information in the grammar box and then to do the exercises.

● The main purpose of this activity is to provide a context for forming the present perfect continuous in a drill-like way. Do this activity in writing, because the sentences will be used in *Sounds* activity 1.

> **Answers**
> 1 since **Thursday**
> 2 for **six** months
> 3 since early this **morning**
> 4 for **two** hours
> 5 since **Tuesday**
> 6 for **ten** hours

2 Aim: to focus on the use of the present perfect continuous.

● Ask the students to rewrite the sentences using the present perfect continuous so that they mean the same.

> **Answers**
> 1 The sun **has been shining** for three hours.
> 2 He**'s been working** for the same company since 1956.
> 3 She**'s been living** with him since 1965.
> 4 We**'ve been going** to Majorca on holiday for ten years.
> 5 I**'ve been learning** Italian since 1987.
> 6 Prices **have been rising** for three months.

3 Aim: to practise forming questions with *how long* and the present perfect continuous; to focus on the use of *for* and *since*.

● Ask the students to write questions using the prompts and the present perfect continuous.

> **Answers**
> 1 How long have you been doing this lesson?
> 2 How long have you been using this book?
> 3 How long have you been learning English?
> 4 How long have you been living in your town?

4 Aim: to practise asking and answering questions in the present perfect continuous; to practise using *since*.

● Ask the students to go round the class asking and answering the questions they wrote in activity 3. Check that everyone is using *since* correctly. Encourage students to note down other students' answers.

5 Aim: to practise writing sentences using the present perfect continuous and *for*.

● Ask the students to write sentences about the other students' answers to activity 4 using *for*.

SOUNDS

1 Aim: to practise contrastive stress in sentences.

● ▱ Explain that information which is corrected is usually stressed strongly. Ask the students to look at the sentences they wrote in *Grammar* activity 1, then play the tape.

● Ask the students in turn to repeat the sentences, making sure they stress the corrected information.

2 Aim: to focus on word stress in sentences.

● Remind the students that in English the speaker stresses the words he or she considers to be important. This means that the stressed words may vary. However, the important words in a news item are fairly predictable, so students should be able to do this activity by simply considering which are the key words in the broadcast.

> **Answers**
> Hijackers are still holding twenty-three passengers in a plane at Manchester airport. They hijacked the flight from London to Glasgow last Thursday. The hostages have now been sitting in the plane without food or water for three days.

● The activity will have a positive effect on both the students' listening comprehension and their pronunciation.

WRITING AND SPEAKING

1 Aim: to practise writing; to practise listening for main ideas.

● ▱ Ask the students to listen to one of the news items and to write down as much as they can without stopping. Do not play the tape a second time at this stage.

● Ask the students to compare their versions with each other. Emphasise that they should try and get a version which is as close as possible to what they heard.

● You may like to play the tape a second time.

● Ask the students to turn to Communication activity 7 on page 99 for their instructions.

2 Aim: to prepare for the speaking activity in 3.

● Ask the students to read the statements and to think about their opinions.

3 Aim: to practise speaking.

● Ask the students to work in small groups. They should discuss their opinions of the statements in 2 with the others. Ask them to choose a spokesperson to report their opinions to the rest of the class.

● Ask the spokespersons from each group to report back its opinions to the rest of the class.

● Open up the discussion for the whole class.

● Note that the issues which concern the media (radio, television, the press etc) will be dealt with in Lesson 24.

13

GENERAL COMMENTS

Present perfect simple and continuous

This lesson's grammar focus is a comparison of the uses of the present perfect simple and continuous.

The explanation in the grammar box is quite succinct for reasons of space, so you may want to draw your students' attention to the Grammar Review at the back of their student's book. Remember that although it is satisfying for students to use the structures accurately and appropriately, misuse rarely causes problems of communication. There is also the risk that the language used to describe the form and meaning of a structure is more complex than the structure itself.

READING

1 Aim: to prepare for reading.

● Ask the students to tell you if they have a favourite TV, film or cartoon character.

● Ask the students to think of as many fictional heroes as they can, such as *Asterix, Batman, Popeye, Lucky Luke, Sherlock Holmes, Tintin, Sinbad, Mickey Mouse, Donald Duck,* and *Roger Rabbit.* Write their names on the board. Who are the most popular cartoon characters in your students' countries?

● Ask the students to look at their books and to match the names with the photos.

● Explain that the idea of these fictional heroes is that they have been around for some time and are likely to be around in the future. This is the focus of the use of the present perfect continuous in this lesson.

2 Aim: to practise reading for main ideas.

● Ask the students to read the passage and to match the names with the paragraphs. Try to dissuade them from asking about specific vocabulary problems for the moment.

Answers
1 James Bond   2 Batman   3 Charlie Brown
4 Bugs Bunny   5 Kermit

3 Aim: to provide an opportunity for a second reading; to focus on the information required to distinguish between present perfect simple and continuous.

● You can either ask students to do this activity orally in small groups or you can do it with the whole class. Dissuade students from writing the answers as they will do this in *Grammar* activity 2 and 3. The answers for your reference are in *Grammar* activities 2 and 3.

● It may be useful at this stage to check on difficult vocabulary. Restrict the number of words you explain to five or six. Encourage the students to explain difficult words themselves.

GRAMMAR

1 Aim: to focus on the form of the present perfect continuous.

● Ask the students to read the information in the grammar box and then to do the exercises.

● Ask the students to say how the present perfect continuous is formed. Remind them, if necessary, that it was presented in Lesson 12.

● Ask the students to read the passage again and to note down the examples of the present perfect continuous.

> **Answers**
> 1 has been working
> 2 has been fighting
> 3 has been living
> 4 has been eating
> 5 has been singing and dancing

2 Aim: to practise using the present perfect continuous and *for* and *since*.

● Ask the students to look at questions 1 to 4 in *Reading* activity 3. Make sure they write full answers to these questions in order to practise the structure. Draw their attention to *How long...* which gives a clue that the present perfect continuous should be used.

> **Answers**
> 1 Batman **has been saving** Gotham City from evil since 1939/for over fifty years.
> 2 Charlie Brown **has been living** in a small American town since 1950/for over forty years.
> 3 Bugs Bunny **has been eating** carrots in public since 1937/for over fifty years.
> 4 Kermit **has been singing** and **dancing** on TV since 1957/for over thirty years.

3 Aim: to focus on the difference between the present perfect simple and continuous.

● Ask the students to look at questions 5 to 8 in *Reading* activity 3. Explain that they should be answered using the present perfect simple. Draw attention to the clue *How much/many...* which suggests that the present perfect simple should be used.

> **Answers**
> 5 They**'ve made** three Batman TV series.
> 6 There **have been** three Charlie Brown films.
> 7 Bugs Bunny **has appeared** in hundreds of cartoon films.
> 8 People **have seen** hundreds of Muppet shows.

4 Aim: to provide further practise in identifying the difference between present perfect simple and continuous.

● Ask students to read the sentences and choose the best verb form.

> **Answers**
> 1 I**'ve been working** for several hours and I still **haven't finished.**
> 2 She**'s been waiting** for thirty minutes and the bus still **hasn't arrived.**
> 3 I**'ve been reading** while she**'s been seeing** the doctor.
> 4 He**'s been talking** to his girlfriend for over an hour. That's the sixth phone call he**'s made** this evening.

VOCABULARY

Aim: to present the vocabulary in the box.

● Ask the students to look at the words in the vocabulary box, and check that they know the meanings. Ask other students to explain any difficult words.

● Say each word in turn and ask the students to try and remember the sentence in which it can be found.

SPEAKING AND WRITING

1 Aim: to practise speaking and writing.

● Write on the board some information about yourself today, for example, *married, teacher of English, live in Stockholm.*

● Write some of the events which relate to your present day life. Some of these could be fictional.
1989 - got married, 1994 - climbed Mount Everest, 1995 - moved to Stockholm

● Ask the students to write similar information about themselves but to include some fictional information.

2 Aim: to practise speaking.

● Ask the students to work together and talk about each others' important events and dates. They should make notes as they listen.

3 To practise writing; to practise using the present perfect simple and continuous.

● Ask each student to work alone and write a biography of their partner, using the relevant tenses.

● You may like to ask the students to do this activity for homework.

4 Aim: to practise reading.

● Ask the students to share their biographies and to look for the false pieces of information.

● Read the most humorous or outrageous biographies to the whole class.

14

GENERAL COMMENTS

Vocabulary

There is quite a lot of vocabulary presented in the boxes in this lesson, although much of it will be revision. There is probably too much for the students to learn in one go, so you may need to help them be selective about the words they record. Nevertheless, the words are presented in the vocabulary boxes because the students should at least be acquainted with them at this level.

Geographical locations

The towns and regions described in *Reward* are chosen in order to emphasise the multi-national context of learning English. It is also hoped that some of the students will come from these places, as students enjoy seeing their home town or country portrayed in a textbook. It should also be pointed out that locations such as London are as much part of this international feel to the series as the presentation of a target culture within the traditional teaching of British life and institutions.

VOCABULARY AND LISTENING

1 Aim: to present the vocabulary in the box; to prepare for listening.

● Ask the students to think of the town where they are now and to suggest words which can be used to describe it. Do the words give a positive or negative impression? Write some of their suggested words on the board.

● Ask the students to look at the words in the vocabulary box. They may recognise some of these words. Ask them to underline the adjectives and say which ones are also nouns.

> **Answers**
> busy, cosmopolitan, crowded, dangerous, dirty, hilly, industrial, lively, noisy, old-fashioned, picturesque, romantic, sleepy, smart, square, unique, wealthy
>
> *Square* is the only adjective here that can be used as a noun.

2 Aim: to practise using the adjectives in the box.

● Ask the students to say which adjectives they can use to describe their own town.

● You may like to extend the activity by asking them to describe other well-known towns and cities with the words, for example, *Paris – wealthy, romantic...*

3 Aim: to practise using the nouns in the box; to focus on collocation.

● Ask the students to talk about their town or a favourite city and to use the nouns in the box to describe it. Encourage them to choose suitable adjectives which go with the nouns as well.

4 Aim: to practise listening and inferring.

● Tell the students they are going to listen to Richard talking about Prague. Ask them to say which adjectives Richard might use to talk about Prague. Write them on the board.

● Ask the students to listen and decide if Richard uses the same adjectives. Does Richard like Prague or not? Play the tape.

> **Answers**
> beautiful, fantastic, wonderful, popular, hot, cold, cheap, clean, romantic

5 Aim: to present the language of making comparisons; to check listening comprehension.

● The answers to this activity provide the information necessary for the functions exercises, and will be exploited more fully in *Functions* activity 2. Students may like to work in pairs for this activity. Encourage them to talk about the details of what was said.

● Play the tape again and check.

> **Answers**
> **age:** old city – but age not specified
> **population:** 1.2 million (smaller than London)
> **industry:** not much, a little on the edge of the city, but nothing in the centre
> **climate:** very hot in the summer, very cold in the winter
> **prices:** quite cheap for British people, a beer costs about 15 pence
> **architecture:** full of wonderful baroque and Gothic buildings
> **transport:** doesn't say
> **cleanliness:** it's a very clean city, hardly any rubbish
> **safety:** you feel safe when you walk the streets at night
> **atmosphere:** romantic
> **culture:** doesn't say – but we can presume it is a cultural city by his comments on architecture
> **entertainment:** doesn't say

GRAMMAR AND FUNCTIONS

1 Aim: to revise comparative and superlative adjectives.

● Ask the students to read the information in the grammar and functions box and then do the exercises.

> **Answers**
> busier – busiest
> more cosmopolitan – most cosmopolitan
> more crowded – most crowded
> more dangerous – most dangerous
> dirtier – dirtiest
> hillier – hilliest
> more industrial – most industrial
> livelier – liveliest
> noisier – noisiest
> more old-fashioned – most old-fashioned
> more picturesque – most picturesque
> more romantic – most romantic
> sleepier – sleepiest
> smarter – smartest
> more unique – most unique
> wealthier – wealthiest
>
> It would be unusual to use a comparative or superlative form of the adjective *square*.

2 Aim: to practise making comparisons.

● Suggest that the students refer to their answers to *Vocabulary and listening* activity 4 and 5.

> **Answers**
> Fewer people live in Prague than in London.
> There's less industry in Prague than in London.
> It's hotter in summer and colder in winter in Prague.
> It's cheaper in Prague than in London.
> It's dirtier in London than in Prague.
> It's less dangerous in Prague than in London.
> It's more romantic in Prague than in London.

READING AND WRITING

1 Aim: to practise reading for specific information.

● Ask the students to read the passage and find which aspects it mentions.

● Check the students' answers to this activity orally.

> **Answers**
> The passage mentions age, population, transport, atmosphere, entertainment, architecture

2 Aim: to practise distinguishing between fact and opinion.

● You may like to ask the students to do this activity together as there may be some useful discussion in deciding which words turn a fact into an opinion.

> **Answers**
> **Facts:** over a thousand years old, population 1,250,000, Gothic and baroque buildings, trams and underground, medieval centre, classical concerts, music festival, tall skyscrapers in suburbs, villages and hills in Bohemia.
>
> **Opinions:** wonderful tower, easy to walk round, many memorable sights, lively atmosphere, delight to visit at any time of year, nowhere quite like Prague.

3 Aim: to prepare for writing; to practise speaking; to practise making comparisons.

● Explain that many cities are twinned with other cities around the world, and the twinning arrangement is based on the similarity in the features mentioned in activity 1. If your students come from Prague or the Czech Republic, ask them if there are other cities which they know well and which are similar to Prague.

● Ask the students to think about towns which could be twinned with Prague.

● Now ask the students to think about the similarities and differences between Prague and the town they have chosen. Go round and check that everyone is making suitable notes. If students know the same city, they can work together.

4 Aim: to practise writing; to present *the main reason why, another reason is, both ... and, neither... nor, while, whereas, but, actually.*

● Check that the students have seen these expressions before. Ask them to use them in a paragraph describing similarities and differences in Prague and the town they have chosen.

● You may like to ask your students to do this activity for homework.

15

GENERAL COMMENTS

Vocabulary work

In *Reward*, the main tasks which accompany the reading and listening passages are designed to bring the students to an understanding of what the passage is about or why it was written. So with a story, for example, the tasks will help the students understand what the plot is about. If there are any vocabulary difficulties which get in the way of comprehension and the ability to complete the task successfully, these will be dealt with either as one of the main tasks or through pre-teaching, usually by including the new words in the vocabulary boxes. The first activity in *Vocabulary and reading* is an example of this. It may be suitable to follow up the main tasks with secondary tasks which develop another aspect of the student's language competence. In activity 4, there is a vocabulary activity which encourages the students to work out the meaning of difficult words for themselves. This is a particularly important skill to develop and one that becomes very relevant to the intermediate learner. So it is not the words in this activity which need to be learnt but the skill of dealing with difficult words. When the students start to become less reliant on the dictionary or your own explanations of the meaning of difficult vocabulary, they start to become fluent readers and listeners of English.

Order of adjectives

The order in which a series of adjectives comes before a noun is quite important, and the rules are easily presented but quickly forgotten. In real-life speech, however, few nouns will have more than two or three adjectives in front of them (in attributive position). Your students may be reassured to learn that many sentences can be reorganised so that the adjectives come after a verb (in predicative position), for example in subordinate or relative clauses, and indeed this is more common in spoken English.

Preparation

Bring a collection of 10 to 20 portable household objects and a large cloth to cover them all.

VOCABULARY AND READING

1 Aim: to present the words in the vocabulary box; to present compound nouns.

● Many European languages do not form compound nouns in the same way as English does. You may need to explain that the second word in a compound noun acts like a noun, and the first word like an adjective. The first noun often says what kind the second noun is. This means that in plural forms the *-s* ending is only placed on the second noun. Explain that these words are either written as one word or two words, and some are written with a hyphen. There are no clear rules on this and the formation should be noted at the time the words are learnt.

● Ask students to look at the vocabulary box and find examples of compound nouns.

> **Answers**
> **one word formed from two nouns:** armchair, ashtray, necklace, wristwatch
> **two words formed from two nouns:** alarm clock, coffee cup, engagement ring, fountain pen, picnic basket

2 Aim: to practise using the words in the vocabulary box; to focus on collocation.

● Start this activity by telling the students which of the words in the box are objects you own.

● Ask the students to put adjectives with the nouns. Help them to focus on the most common combinations. For example, *an antique silver candlestick* is a more common combination, but *an antique silver alarm clock* would be more surprising.

3 Aim: to practise reading for specific information.

● The students should now be well-prepared for the reading activity. Ask them to read and find the objects which answer the questions. Not all the nouns are in the vocabulary box. Elicit the missing words from the students.

> **Answers**
> **nouns in the box:** bicycle, coffee cup, fountain pen, engagement ring, ashtray
> **nouns not in the box:** remote control, eighteenth-century prints, airplanes

4 Aim: to practise dealing with unfamiliar words.

● The questions in this activity are designed to help the students guess the general sense of unfamiliar words rather than their exact meaning. Try to resist giving a detailed explanation or translation as the words and expressions are not essential for productive use at this level.

● Encourage the students to look for clues in the context of the passage to help them.

GRAMMAR

1 Aim: to focus on the order of adjectives.

● Ask the students to read the information in the grammar box and then to do the exercises.

● You may like to ask the students to do this activity orally.

Answers
1 A charming, round, wooden dining table.
2 A smart, white, Italian sports car.
3 A large, old, brown paper bag.
4 Two comfortable, English, leather armchairs.
5 Fine German, sparkling wine.

2 Aim: to practise placing adjectives in the right order.

● Ask the students to do this activity in pairs. Refer the students back to the possessions they made notes on or talked about in *Vocabulary and reading* activity 2 and ask them to write sentences describing them.

● Ask the students to read out some of the sentences they have written.

3 Aim: to practise using possessive pronouns and adjectives.

● Give the students time to do this activity on their own, and then check their answers orally.

Answers
1 your, mine
2 my, yours
3 our, theirs
4 her, my
5 your, my

SOUNDS

1 Aim: to focus on stress in compound nouns.

● 📼 This activity focuses on the general rule concerning stress in compound nouns, which is that the stress is usually on the first noun. But there will be exceptions, and even difference between British and American usage.

Answers
<u>alarm</u> clock, <u>coffee</u> cup, <u>fountain</u> pen, <u>ash</u>tray, <u>hair</u>brush, <u>picnic</u> basket, <u>wrist</u>watch

● Ask the students to say the words aloud.

SPEAKING

1 Aim: to practise speaking; to review the vocabulary presented in this lesson.

● Refer the students back to the text and ask them to talk about their answers to the questions. Encourage them to describe their possessions in great detail using as many adjectives as possible. Remind them that they used these adjectives to describe their possessions in *Grammar* activity 2.

● Ask the students to work in groups and to choose three or four items or favourite things. They should write down the word for the item or favourite thing and underneath these words, the adjectives which they can use to describe them.

2 Aim: to practise speaking; to practise using adjectives in the correct order, possessive pronouns and possessive adjectives.

● This is a variation on the children's game called *Kim's game*. Ask the students to work in pairs or small groups.

● Place the objects you brought into the class in front of the students and ask them to study the objects carefully for about thirty seconds. Then cover the objects with a cloth or a coat.

● Then ask the students to write down as many objects as possible. Encourage them to describe them in detail, using adjectives in the right order.

Progress check 11–15

GENERAL COMMENTS

You can work through this Progress check in the order shown, or concentrate on areas which may have caused difficulty in Lessons 11 to 15. You can also let the students choose the activities they would like to or feel the need to do.

VOCABULARY

1 **Aim: to focus on adjective + particles.**

● Explain that the adjectives presented in this activity need to be followed by a particular particle. The particle should be noted at the time of learning, if possible.

> **Answers**
> accustomed to, afraid of, allergic to,
> angry with, bored with, capable of, certain to,
> confident of, fond of, frightened of, in love with,
> pleased with, proud of, related to, similar to,
> typical of

2 **Aim: to practise using adjective + particles.**

> **Answers**
> 1 She didn't like swimming because she was **afraid of** water.
> 2 Your teacher is very **pleased with** your hard work.
> 3 After several years, she grew **accustomed to** his strange behaviour.
> 4 I am **confident of** her support in the election.
> 5 She was **allergic to** cats.
> 6 It was **typical of** him to lose his temper.

3 **Aim: to focus on adjectives which can only go in predicative position.**

● Remind the students that some adjectives can only go after a verb and not before a noun. The most common verbs used for predicative adjectives are *be, seem, look*, and *become*.

> **Answers**
> afraid, alive, alone, apart, aware, glad, ill, likely (to),
> ready, sorry, sure, unable (to)

4 **Aim: to help the students organise their vocabulary learning.**

● Remind the students that they need to go back over their *Wordbanks* every so often. It also maybe helpful to organise the words in different categories.

GRAMMAR

1 **Aim: to revise *already, yet* and *still*.**

> **Answers**
> 1 yet, still
> 2 already
> 3 yet, still
> 4 still
> 5 yet
> 6 already, yet

2 **Aim: to revise present perfect continuous and *for* and *since*.**

> **Answers**
> 1 It**'s been raining** for an hour.
> 2 I**'ve been living** in this flat for twenty years.
>   I**'ve been living** in this flat since 1975.
> 3 I**'ve been waiting** for a bus for twenty minutes.
> 4 They**'ve been building** the house for three months.
> 5 She**'s been standing** there for ten minutes.
> 6 He**'s been painting** the room for a week.
>   He**'s been painting** the room since last week.

3 **Aim: to revise the difference between the present perfect simple and continuous.**

> **Answers**
> haven't seen
> have you been
> have you been working
> have been running
> has been getting
> have you moved
> have moved

4 Aim: to revise ways of making comparisons.

Answers
1 New York is bigger than Paris.
2 In Spain there are more tourists than in Britain.
3 In Germany there is more industry than in Portugal.
4 Paris is more beautiful than London.
5 New York is more dangerous than Madrid.
6 In London there is more rain than in Manchester.

5 Aim: to revise the order of adjectives.
● Ask the students to describe their possessions in as much detail as possible.

6 Aim: to revise possessive pronouns and adjectives.

Answers
1 my
2 her, theirs
3 our, yours
4 their, their
5 our, mine
6 my, your

SOUNDS

1 Aim: to focus on consonant clusters in initial position and final position.
● 🔲 Speakers of certain languages have difficulties with words with consonant clusters in initial and final position. Ask the students to say the words aloud. Help them correct their pronunciation if necessary. You may find it useful to play the tape and stop after each word.

2 Aim: to focus on linked sounds in connected speech.
● It is unlikely that your students will use the rules to produce linked sounds in connected speech, as they are rather complex. Use the activity simply to make them aware of the linked sounds when they're listening. It may be that the linked sounds are very common in everyday English but may sometimes make it more difficult to understand fluent speakers of English.

3 Aim: to revise word stress in sentences.

● In Lesson 12, it was pointed out that news bulletins can provide a fairly predictable stress pattern, as it is fairly obvious which are the most important words. Ask the students to predict which words are likely to be stressed.

● 🔲 Play the tape and ask them to check their answers.

Answer
A <u>demonstration</u> against <u>unemployment</u> has been taking place in <u>Manchester</u>. <u>Demonstrators</u> have been <u>marching</u> through the city for <u>two</u> hours. It is expected to <u>finish</u> in front of the <u>town hall</u> at <u>five</u> this <u>evening</u> where <u>left-wing</u> Members of <u>Parliament</u> will <u>address</u> the <u>crowd</u>.

SPEAKING

Aim: to practise speaking; to review the vocabulary used to describe objects in Lessons 11 to 15.
● This activity is meant to be light-hearted and will involve some movement, if possible. Ask the students to work in groups of three or four and to follow the instructions.

● Here are some phrases which you can whisper to the students from each group.
1 *pick up the children*
2 *prime minister*
3 *Kermit the frog*
4 *a romantic city*
5 *brand-new mountain bike*

● You can add further phrases taken from Lessons 11 to 15.

16

GENERAL COMMENTS

Topics

One of the most popular topics in the classroom is fashion and style. Use this lesson to explore this motivating subject fully, by encouraging the students to talk about clothes, behaviour, activities, films etc which are in fashion at the moment.

A Year in Provence

The passage is an extract from Peter Mayle's book *A Year in Provence*. Peter Mayle worked in advertising in London until one day he and his wife decided to move to the south of France. The book is a detailed and often amusing description of the first year in their new home, and an account of the difficulties that foreigners may have when they try to assimilate themselves into a new culture. Ironically, the book has been so famous that visitors looking for Peter Mayle's Provence have destroyed the peace and quiet which he describes in his book.

VOCABULARY

1 Aim: to present the words in the vocabulary box.

- To present some of the more obscure words, ask the students about their clothing, hairstyle, accessories etc.

- Explain that *accessories* are items which you wear or carry but which are not part of the main clothing. Some students may not agree that a baseball cap or a bow tie is an item of clothing and not an accessory. Ask the students to put the words in categories.

> **Answers**
> **Hair:** crew cut, ponytail
> **Face:** beard, moustache, stubble
> **Clothes:** baseball cap, bikini, boxer shorts, bow tie, cardigan, flares, flip-flops, high heels, leather jacket, sandals, T-shirt, vest, waistcoat
> **Accessories:** belt, earrings, handbag, sunglasses

2 Aim: to present the words in the vocabulary box.

- It is very common when talking about fashion to use words which describe shades of different colours rather than the colours themselves. Ask the students if this is true in their own language. If you all share the same language, make a list of words to describe different shades.

- Ask the students to match the shades in the box and the colours. Explain that some shades may come from two different colours.

- Ask students to turn to Communication activity 15 on page 102 to check.

3 Aim: to present the words in the vocabulary box.

- The words all refer to different materials which may or may not be fashionable at the moment. Think of common things which are made in the different materials to illustrate their meaning. For example, *leather jacket, cotton shirt, linen suit, silk scarf, canvas shoes, towelling bathrobe, wool sweater, denim jeans.*

- Ask the students to work in small groups and to talk about fashionable clothes, accessories, colours and materials.

- Find out who is the most fashion-conscious in the class. Why do they think being fashionable is important?

READING

1 Aim: to read for main ideas.

● The general nature of the reading task in this activity should ensure that the students read the passage for its main ideas and not concentrate on the meaning of individual words at this stage.

> **Answer**
> The writer's advice is mainly for women.

2 Aim: to focus on the writer's style.

● Find out if the students think the passage is meant to be taken seriously or not. Do they think the advice given is relevant to people who want to be fashionable and stylish today?

> **Possible answer**
> humorous, ironic

3 Aim: to focus on techniques for understanding the general sense of difficult words.

● Explain that it isn't necessary to learn the meaning of the words featured in this activity, but that they may be needed to understand the general sense of the passage. Work through this activity with the whole class.

● The students may want to find an exact meaning for these words. There's no need to discourage them from doing so, but it may be better to ensure that they do not note down the words in their *Wordbanks*.

FUNCTIONS AND GRAMMAR

1 Aim: to practise using the target grammar and functions.

● Ask the students to read the explanation in the functions and grammar box and then do the activities.

● You may like to start this activity with the whole class. Encourage everyone to think of advice for the different situations.

● Ask the students to work in pairs or small groups and to discuss the situations. They may like to make some notes.

● Ask the whole class to give their advice, and write it on the board.

2 Aim: to practise using the target grammar and functions.

● Complete these practice activities by asking students to think about doing things in style. Ask them to write sentences giving their advice.

● Ask the students to read out their advice to the whole class. Who gives the best advice?

SPEAKING AND WRITING

1 Aim: to practise speaking; to prepare for writing.

● Continue the discussion about fashion which you started in *Vocabulary* activity 3 by asking students about other fashions and trends at the moment.

2 Aim: to practise writing.

● Ask the students to write some advice for visitors to their country. They may enjoy this activity more if they imagine they have a penfriend in a foreign country or know someone who lives abroad. They may like to write an informal letter to them giving their advice.

● You may like to ask the students to do this activity for homework.

17

GENERAL COMMENTS

Stories

Reward Intermediate contains a number of short stories presented in listening or reading form. Everyone enjoys stories, although not everyone will necessarily enjoy the same story. But one of the most popular genres is thrillers so there is a chance that the ghost story in this lesson will appeal to a substantial number of students. In the classroom, the students read and listen in a way that they would not usually do in real life: they are told what to read or listen to, they are not allowed to abandon the text until they have finished, and there are all sorts of tasks accompanying the text. Of course, if the story is interesting enough, it would be better for it not to be accompanied by any task because the motivation to read or listen would be enough to create the best circumstances for reading practice. In a textbook lesson, however, there are a number of objectives other than skills development, and in *Reward* the main focus of each lesson is the grammar and vocabulary. So *Rose Rose* has been chosen because there's a good chance that the students will enjoy it, but the accompanying tasks are designed to create artificial motivation to listen if the authentic motivation is missing, and to meet the other objectives of the lesson.

● Write on the board some newspaper headlines about important items of news, current events or the weather today. Ask the students to talk about what they think each news item might be about.

● Ask if they think any of them will change in the next few days, and if so, what might happen. The language they need for this is the target grammar of the lesson, which should mostly be revision.

● Ask them to imagine the headlines about the same items of news etc in a few days' time. What might they say?

FUNCTIONS AND GRAMMAR

1 Aim: to present and practise ways of making predictions.

● Ask the students to read the information in the functions and grammar box and then to do the exercises.

● Exceptionally, the grammar is presented at the start of the lesson, because the structures are required for the successful completion of the tasks in the rest of the material. Ask the students to read the sentences and to choose the best form of the verb. Point out that if something is arranged, then a verb which expresses certainty is required. If it isn't arranged, then a structure implying probability or possibility can be used. Point out that *may, might* and *will* are modal verbs: they have the same form in all persons, they don't use *do* in the negative and they take an infinitive without *to*.

> **Answers**
> 1 I **won't** be in at nine tomorrow as I have a dentist's appointment at that time.
> 2 There are no buses after midnight, and it's too far to walk so I **will** take a taxi.
> 3 She **might** come and stay at Christmas or she may stay at home.
> 4 I'm thinking of seeing some friends tonight, so I definitely **won't** be back at seven.
> 5 They**'re going** to the theatre tonight. They've got tickets.

2 Aim: to practise making predictions.

● Ask the students to work alone for this activity and write down a few predictions.

● Ask the students to work in pairs and to talk about their predictions.

3 Aim: to practise using *going to* and *will*.

● Write on the board the following sentences: *My hair's too long. My car won't start. My flat is in a mess,* or any other sentences which describe present situations in your personal life. Tell the class what you'll do about each one, for example, *I know! I'll go to the hairdresser.*

● Ask one or two students to tell the rest of the class what you've decided to do. Make sure they use *going to*: *She's going to the hairdresser.*

● Ask the students to write down three decisions. Remind them that they use *will* to describe the decision at the moment they make it.

● Ask the students to tell each other about their decisions. Check that they use *going to*.

LISTENING AND SPEAKING

1 Aim: to prepare for listening; to practise making predictions.
● This activity will require the language of making predictions. Ask the students to look at the picture and to predict what the story might be about and what type of story it might be. Make sure they use the structures presented in the functions and grammar box.

2 Aim: to prepare for listening; to practise making predictions.
● Tell the students that the sentences are all spoken by one of the two characters. Ask them to identify the two characters in the picture.

● Ask the students to predict who says the sentences. Once again, make sure they use the structures in the functions and grammar box. Ask them to explain which words helped them make up their minds. The activity will also help the students prepare for listening.

> **Answers**
> a Sefton b Sefton c Miss Rose d Miss Rose
> e Sefton f Miss Rose g Sefton

3 Aim: to practise listening for main ideas.
● ⊟ Play the tape and ask the students simply to number the sentences as they hear them.

> **Answers**
> b 1 f 2 g 3 a 4 e 5 d 6 c 7

● Check that everyone has understood the main ideas by asking one or two students to re-tell the story to the rest of the class. You may like to play the story a second time at this stage.

4 Aim: to prepare for listening; to practise making predictions.
● Explain that the answers to the questions will provide a framework of the plot for the next part of the story. Ask the students to work in pairs, to read the questions and to predict what the answers might be. You may like to ask them to write full answers to the questions, but leaving out anything they can't guess. The answers are in activity 5.

5 Aim: to practise listening for main ideas.
● ⊟ Ask the students to listen and check their answers to 4.

> **Answers**
> 1 He was at his studio by half-past eight.
> 2 Because they both distrust each other.
>   3 He went to the tobacconist on the corner.
> 4 He expected her to arrive twenty minutes late.
> 5 She arrives on time.
> 6 He felt human fingers drawn lightly across the back of his neck.
> 7 Miss Rose had disappeared.
> 8 He was very frightened.
> 9 He read that Miss Rose, an artist's model, had been knocked down by a car in the Fulham Road about seven o'clock on the previous evening; that the owner of the car had stopped and taken her to hospital, and that she had died within a few minutes of admission.
> 10 He opened it and stood in front of the picture. We don't know exactly what he's going to do.

● Ask the students to discuss what they think Sefton does next.

VOCABULARY AND WRITING

1 Aim: to present the vocabulary in the box; to exploit the vocabulary generated by the text.
● Check that the students understand the words in the story. Can they remember the sentence in which the words appeared?

● Ask the students to read the tapescript and see if there are any other words which they would like to add to their lists.

2 Aim: to practise writing; to present *although* and *in spite of*.
● Ask the students to talk about the story and to imagine the ending. Suggest that they rewrite the story from Miss Rose's point of view. Help them to use the linking words to contrast ideas.

● Ask the students to write the endings of their stories for homework. If you do this, you may like to stop them looking at the ending in the Communication activity.

3 Aim: to practise reading for main ideas; to react to the text.
● The Communication activity 8 on page 99 contains the real ending to the story. Ask the students to read it and to discuss if they find it better than their own endings.

18

Motivation

There are three factors which the textbook can contribute towards motivating the students: topic, texts and tasks. Ideally, the topic of the lesson needs to be something that interests the students enough to talk about not only during the lesson but also outside the classroom. There will, however, be some topics which will be less appealing but which still have to be dealt with because they represent important lexical fields. The texts in a textbook are chosen because of their potential intrinsic interest, and care is taken to avoid telling the students something they already know just because it happens to be in English. Texts with personal relevance to the students, with entertainment value, of a suitable length, and of an attractive appearance are included in *Reward*. But not every text is going to appeal to every student all of the time. In these circumstances, the task should supplement the motivation that the topic or text might lack. In the *Reading and speaking* section of this lesson, there is a text organisation activity, known as dovetailed texts, because this micro skill generates a number of interesting and motivating activities.

VOCABULARY AND SPEAKING

1 Aim: to present or revise the vocabulary in the box.

● Ask the students *What do you do?* or, depending on the age of your students, *What would you like to be?* and elicit *I'm a.../I'd like to be a...* and a suitable job. Check that they precede it with the indefinite article.

● Ask the students to look at the words in the box and see if they can find a job they would prefer to have, or something they would like to be. If they can't find a job in the vocabulary box, they can suggest some other job.

● Write the words for describing personal and professional qualities on the board. Check that everyone understands all the words.

● Ask them to choose three words to describe their own character. Explain that only three students can use each word. At random, ask students to say the three words they have chosen, and put a tick by the word. When a word has three ticks, other students are not allowed to choose it and have to find another word.

● Carry on until the last student has chosen his/her words. Does the rest of the class think they are suitable words to describe him/her?

● Ask the students to say what qualities and characteristics you need to do the jobs in the vocabulary box.

2 Aim: to read and answer a questionnaire.

● Ask the students to read and answer the questionnaire.

3 Aim: to practise speaking.

● Ask the students to discuss their answers to the questionnaire in pairs.

FUNCTIONS

1 Aim: to practise ways of drawing conclusions.

● Ask the students to read the information in the grammar box and then to do the exercises.

● You may like to do this activity orally with the whole class.

● Ask the students to repeat the activity orally in pairs.

Answers
1 Yes, he **must** be a journalist.
2 No, he **can't** be a doctor.
3 Yes, he **might** be working late.
4 No, she **can't** have a job.
5 Yes, she **must** be able to drive.
6 No, she **can't** be in the office at the moment.
7 Yes, he **might** be a farmer.
8 Yes, she **must** be reliable.

● Ask the students to write their answers because this will be used for *Sounds* activity 2.

2 Aim: to practise ways of describing impressions.

● Ask the students to do this activity in writing.

● You can check this activity orally with the whole class.

SOUNDS

1 Aim: to focus on word stress.
● Ask the students to say the words aloud and to underline the stressed syllable.

● 🔲 Play the tape and ask the students to listen and check.

2 Aim: to focus on strong stress and intonation for disagreeing.
● 🔲 Point out that when you disagree with someone, you stress the information about which you disagree. This can also have an effect on the intonation. Play the tape and ask the students to listen to the stress and intonation.

● Ask the students to say the sentences aloud.

LISTENING

Aim: to practise listening for main ideas.
● 🔲 Explain that three people will be talking about their answers to the questionnaire. None of them know, and therefore have to guess, what each other's job is. Play the tape and stop after every three or four questions to see if the students can guess what the three jobs are.

READING

1 Aim: to practise reading for main ideas.

● This dovetailed text activity will involve some careful, close reading, but the students are not required to separate the two texts until the next activity. Ask them to read it and find the job which each of the two speakers have.

2 Aim: to practise reading for understanding text organisation.
● Ask the students to read and separate the two texts.

● Ask the students to check their answers with another student.

● For homework, you may like to ask the students to write about a job without mentioning its name. You can then display the texts during the next lesson and ask the students to guess what the jobs are.

19

GENERAL COMMENTS

Talking about obligation

This lesson continues the work begun in Lesson 16 on talking about obligation, and focuses on rules imposed by some external authority, as opposed to a personal or moral obligation. It is hoped that the interest generated by the photos and the topic of the Way of St James will allow the target structure to be dealt with in an unusual way.

Controversial topics

Textbooks try to cater for the general interests, opinions and beliefs of students as a group according to their level and age. It is not able to do the same for individuals. There are some topics that may generate controversy in the classroom between individual students, and these are topics which are not best dealt with in a textbook. Religion and politics are two potentially controversial topics which may need to be handled carefully by the teacher in order to respect the individual sensitivities of the students. The textbook needs to create an opportunity to cover these topics, as they represent important lexical fields, but the teacher should manage any discussions with sensitivity.

VOCABULARY AND READING

1 Aim: to introduce the topic of the lesson; to present the vocabulary in the box; to pre-teach some useful words.

● Ask the students to keep their books closed, and write the words in the vocabulary box on the board. Explain that the words come from the passage they are going to read. They can all be categorised under two headings. Can they decide what the headings might be?

● Ask the students to check their answers with another student.

● Ask the students to open their books and to check. Did they decide correctly? Do they need to categorise the words differently?

> **Answers**
> **religion:** cathedral, church, incense, pilgrim, priest, saint, statue, temptation
>
> **tourism:** backpack, bicycle, hitchhike, holiday, horseback, hostel, package tour, shell, sightseeing, souvenirs, stamp, walker

2 Aim: to practise reading for main ideas.

● The task in this activity is designed to distract the students from attempting to find out the meaning of every unfamiliar word. If they have difficulty with the text, ask the students to work in groups of three and to explain or find out the meanings of difficult words. Then divide the group into Student A, Student B and Student C. Form new groups with Student As, Student Bs and Student Cs. They should tell each other about the difficult words and the explanations which they talked about in their first groups.

● The passage was written by David Lodge, the Catholic novelist, who first suggested the link between tourism and religion in his book *Paradise News*.

> **Answer**
> b

3 Aim: to practise reading for main ideas.

● This activity takes the practice in reading for main ideas one stage further in which the students are encouraged to develop their summary skills. In this carefully graded task, they are simply required to recognise the best summary, not actually write it themselves.

> **Answer**
> 1

● If your students enjoy discussion, ask them if they agree with the writer's main idea.

FUNCTIONS

1 **Aim: to practise talking about obligation, permission and prohibition; to provide an opportunity for a second reading.**

● Ask the students to read the information in the box and then to do the exercises.

● Make it clear to the students that these statements are all false. The aim of the activity is to correct them, using the target structures.

> **Answers**
> 1 You're not allowed to give the pilgrims a lift.
> 2 You're allowed to talk to them.
> 3 They were obliged to travel in groups.
> 4 They had to stay in special hostels.
> 5 They had to travel on foot.
> 6 You have to get a stamp at various places.
> 7 You have to show your passport in Santiago.
> 8 Pilgrims can't eat (their free meal) in the main hotel restaurant.

2 **Aim: to practise talking about obligation and prohibition.**

● You may like to do this exercise orally and with the group as a whole.

● Find out if there are any other rules which the students can think of and express using the target language.

> **Answers**
> 1 You're not allowed to smoke.
> 2 You have to show your tickets.
> 3 You can't take photographs.
> 4 Women have to wear a hat.
> 5 You have to talk quietly.
> 6 You have to remove your shoes.

SOUNDS

Aim: to focus on weak and strong forms.

● You may need to remind the students that weak forms often occur in connected speech. Point out that *have to* is pronounced /hæf tə/ in the first sentence and /hæf tuː/ in the second. Similarly *can* is pronounced /kən/ in the first sentence and /kæn/ in the second.

● Ask the students to say the sentences aloud.

● ▭ Play the tape and ask the students to listen and repeat. Did they say the sentences correctly?

WRITING

1 **Aim: to prepare for writing.**

● Continue the theme of the lesson by asking the students to work in groups of two or three and to write notes on a situation which involves a number of rules. Ask them to make notes, using the suggestions in *Writing* activity 1.

● You may like to prompt the students with the following ideas: *school rules, military service, household rules, driving rules, rules in public places.*

2 **Aim: to practise writing paragraphs; to practise using the linking words for a list of points and for contrasting points.**

● The linking words presented in this activity are often used to make a list of points. You may like to stress the importance of the use of commas to mark the end of the linking words.

● You may like to ask the students to do this activity for homework.

20

GENERAL COMMENTS

Learner training

At this mid-stage lesson in *Reward* Intermediate, the students should be taking a much greater responsibility for their learning. So far, this has been encouraged by creating the opportunity for the students to organise their vocabulary learning according to personal categories, and to select the items which are personally relevant. Careful but effective use of the dictionary should be encouraged at this stage. Every student has different and specific needs, and no single teacher or textbook can hope to meet these personal requirements exactly. It is therefore the student's responsibility to adapt what is presented to them by the teacher and the textbook to their particular circumstances.

Compound adjectives

You may want to explain that there are several possible combinations for forming compound adjectives.
The most common are:
adjective + noun + *-ed*:
> *thick-skinned*

adjective or adverb + past participle:
> *well-behaved*

adjective/adverb or noun + present participle:
> *good-looking*

noun + adjective:
> *world-famous*

Most will have a hyphen between the two parts, but there are some exceptions: *outspoken, outgoing*.

VOCABULARY AND SPEAKING

1 Aim: to introduce the topic.
- The theme of the lesson is assertiveness. Write on the board *Are you assertive?* and find out if anyone thinks they are assertive. What are the advantages and disadvantages of being assertive?

- Ask the students to think about their answers to the questions by answering *yes*, *no* or *sometimes*.

2 Aim: to practise speaking.
- Encourage the students to ask you some of the questions. Give full answers using the language shown in the example. This will give them a model of the language required for this activity.

- Ask two or three students some of the questions in the questionnaire. Elicit answers using *yes* or *no*.

- Ask the students to work in pairs and to talk about their answers to the questions in activity 1.

- Open the activity up to a class discussion.

3 Aim: to present the vocabulary in the box.
- Ask the students to match the adjectives with the questions in the questionnaire. There may be more than one possibility.

> **Answers**
> Can you...
> always tell people what you really think? **outspoken**
> relax with people you don't know? **easy-going**
> usually get what you want? **strong-willed**
> keep calm in stressful situations? **cool-headed**
> keep your temper under control? **cool-headed**
> laugh at yourself? **good-humoured/easy-going**
> always see both sides of an argument? **fair-minded**
> ignore criticism easily? **thick-skinned**
> express your feelings easily? **self-assured** or
> > **outgoing**

- Ask the students to look at the pictures and define the other adjectives in the box. Explain any unfamiliar words with suitable examples. Remind the students how to use defining relative clauses, using the expression *someone who*.

4 Aim: to practise using the vocabulary presented so far; to present the language in the box; to prepare for the grammatical focus.
- The grammar point is concerned with ability and possibility, especially in the past. Ask the students to discuss the general abilities, characteristics and qualities they had as a child.

FUNCTIONS AND GRAMMAR

1 Aim: to focus on *can, could* and *be able to*.

● Ask the students to read the information in the grammar box and then to do the exercises.

● This activity will cause problems if the students are unable to distinguish between a general ability in the past and a possibility on a specific occasion in the past.

> **Answers**
> 1 I know your face but I **can't** remember your name.
> 2 He looked for the book but he **couldn't** find it.
> 3 When he was young, he **could** sing very well.
> 4 She's ill, so she **won't be able** to come this weekend.
> 5 If he spoke slowly, I **could** understand him.
> 6 It was very dangerous, but she **was able to** keep calm.
> 7 She was sensitive and she **couldn't** take criticism.
> 8 I used to **be able** to dance well, but I **couldn't** dance last night.

2 Aim: to practise using *can, could* and *be able to*.

● Ask the students to work in pairs and to follow the instructions. Draw their attention to the fact that it is specific occasions in the past which are being focused on in this activity, so, the relevant structure is likely to be *was/were able to* and *couldn't*.

LISTENING AND WRITING

1 Aim: to prepare for listening; to pre-teach unfamiliar vocabulary.

● Ask the students to look at the words and phrases and to predict what happens in part one of the story. They are in the order in which they will be heard. You may want to point out that Rosalind does not lose her temper in this part. Explain that the words and phrases contain the main ideas of the first part.

● 🔲 Play the tape and ask the students to check their answers.

2 Aim: to check comprehension; to practise the target structures; to provide an opportunity for a second listening.

● Ask the students to read the statements and to look for the false ones. They can do this in pairs if they like.

> **Answers**
> 1 False. Rosalind could drive.
> 2 False. They were able to find a parking space.
> 3 False. They couldn't take the stairs.
> 4 False. Peter was able to walk but not very far.
> 5 True.
> 6 False. They were able to hear the alarm bell.
> 7 False. They couldn't think of much to talk about.
> 8 True.
> 9 False. She couldn't control her temper.
> 10 False. She was able to laugh about it afterwards.

3 Aim: to practise speaking; to prepare for listening.

● Ask the students to predict what happens next. Has anyone ever been in a similar situation?

4 Aim: to practise listening for main ideas; to prepare for activity 5.

● Ask the students to read the phrases.

● 🔲 Play the tape and ask them to listen and put a tick or a cross by the things the people were or weren't able to do. Did they predict correctly in activity 3.

> **Answers**
> get back to the car in time ✗
> join in the argument ✗
> persuade him to take the ticket back ✗
> pay the fine ✓
> keep her temper ✗
> disappear into the crowd ✓
> take the ticket from the windscreen ✓
> control herself ✗

5 Aim: to practise the target structures; to provide an opportunity for a second listening.

● 🔲 Before they listen again, ask the students to check their answers to activity 4, and to try and remember as much detail as possible. Play the tape.

● Ask one student to start re-telling the story. If any other students think he/she has missed out any details, they can ask a question. If he/she gets it right, he/she can continue. If he/she gets it wrong, the other student can take over.

6 Aim: to practise writing a story.

● The collaborative techniques in activities 5 and 6 allow the students to write a full story without having to generate it all on their own. Give them about three or four minutes for this activity.

● Ask the students to pass on their sentences to the student on their right and they will receive the sentences written by the student on their left. They should correct any mistakes and continue with the story.

● If time is short, you can ask them simply to write out the story for homework.

Progress check 16–20

GENERAL COMMENTS

You can work through this Progress check in the order shown, or concentrate on areas which may have caused difficulty in Lessons 16 to 20. You can also let the students choose the activities they would like to or feel the need to do.

VOCABULARY

1 Aim: to present multi-part verbs.

● This is the first time multi-part verbs have been presented in *Reward* Intermediate although by no means the first time the students have come across them. It was decided to use the term *multi-part verbs* as *phrasal verbs* and *prepositional verbs* are terms which are only useful after you know how they operate and where to place the pronoun. This type of verb is extremely common in English and their use often demonstrates fluent, natural speech or writing; they are therefore preferred to Latin-origin verbs.

● Ask the students to work through the explanation and activity.

> **Answers**
> **with object:** take off (before the particle)
> look for (after the particle)
> bring up (before the particle)
> give up (before the particle)
> pull down (before the particle)
> pick up (before the particle)
> give back (before the particle)
> fill in (before the particle)
> turn down (before the particle)
> put off (before the particle)
> **without object:** take off

2 Aim: to focus on the meaning of phrasal verbs.

● Once again remind the students that it is more common in English to use the phrasal verb, even though it is more difficult for students to manipulate.

> **Answers**
> demolish – pull down
> complete – fill in
> lift – pick up
> postpone – put off
> raise – bring up
> reduce – turn down
> remove – take off
> return – give back
> stop – give up
> search for – look for

3 Aim: to focus on the position of the pronoun in sentences with multi-part verbs.

● Ask the students to complete the sentences, taking care over the position of the pronoun.

> **Answers**
> 1 bring it back
> 2 went over the
> 3 join in
> 4 cleared it up
> 5 cut out
> 6 give it all away

4 Aim: to help the students organise their vocabulary learning.

● Remind the students that they need to go back over their *Wordbanks* every so often. It also may be helpful to organise the words in different categories.

GRAMMAR

1 Aim: to revise *will* and *going to*.

> **Answers**
> 1 I'**ll** have some juice.
> 2 It's **going to** rain.
> 3 We're **going to** live in Paris.
> 4 I'**ll** sit down.
> 5 I'm **going to** buy him a present.

2 Aim: to revise drawing conclusions.

> **Answers**
> 1 Yes, she **must** be tired.
> 2 Yes, it **might** be late.
> 3 Yes, he **might** be stuck in the traffic.
> 4 Yes, she **must** live here.
> 5 Yes, he **might** not speak French.
> 6 Yes, she **can't** be home yet.

3 Aim: to revise describing impressions.

> **Answers**
> 1 That armchair looks comfortable.
> 2 It looks heavy.
> 3 He looks like a tourist.
> 4 It sounds like a church.
> 5 He sounds good-humoured.
> 6 He sounds short-tempered.

4 Aim: to revise *should, shouldn't, might, can't, don't have to* and *mustn't*.

> **Answers**
> 1 You **can't** park on a pedestrian crossing.
> 2 You **shouldn't** stay up so late if you're so tired in the morning.
> 3 'Keep off the grass' means that you **can't** walk on the grass.
> 4 You **mustn't** be late for work.
> 5 Thank you for the lift, but I'm afraid you **can't** come in.
> 6 You **mustn't** put your feet on the table.

5 Aim: to revise *can, could* and *be able to*.

> **Answers**
> 1 It was late but luckily we were **able to** get the last bus home.
> 2 If she wrote clearly, I **could** read her handwriting.
> 3 Sorry, **could** you repeat that? I **couldn't** hear what you said.
> 4 He worked very hard and he **was able** to earn a lot of money.
> 5 He was tired, but he **could** stay awake until he got home.
> 6 It was raining so we weren**'t able to** go out.

SOUNDS

1 Aim: to focus on the different ways of pronouncing of the letter *a*.

● The students will already be well aware of the way English can pronounce the same letter in different ways. In the next Progress check lessons, the sounds work will focus on all the vowels, starting with the letter *a*.

● Ask the students to say the words aloud and to put them into groups.

> **Answers**
> /ɔː/: small awful call
> /ɑː/: dark father start
> /æ/: hand flat man
> /eɪ/: take name sale
> /eə/: care rare stare

2 Aim: to focus on *s* + consonant in initial position.

● 📼 Speakers of some languages, such as Spanish, have difficulty in pronouncing *s* + consonant in initial position, and tend to precede it with /e/. If this is not the case with your students, you may like to leave out this activity. If it is the case, play the tape and ask the students to listen and repeat the words.

● Other words which begin with *s* + consonant: *scared, Scandinavia, Scotch, scramble, skinny, sky, smoker, sneeze, speed, spectacular*.

3 Aim: to focus on the /ə/ sound.

● The weak form of vowels or *schwa* is very common in English. Some students may have practised this kind of vowel reduction in *Reward* Pre-intermediate, but this will be the first occasion in this level. Ask them to predict which words are likely to contain *schwa*.

● Ask the students to predict which words will be stressed.

● 📼 Play the tape and ask the students to say the sentences aloud.

> **Answers**
> If you drive across the south-west of France and into northern Spain you'll begin to notice groups of walkers. Most are carrying backpacks and long sticks, and somewhere they're wearing a scallop shell. You can stop and talk to them, but you're not allowed to give them a lift.

SPEAKING AND WRITING

1 Aim: to practise speaking; to practise making deductions and drawing conclusions.

● Ask the students to read the sentences on their own and decide which must be, might be and can't be true.

● Ask the students to check their answers in pairs.

> **Answer**
> All the statements are false.

2 Aim: to practise writing.

● Ask the students to work in pairs, and to write three statements that must be, might be and can't be true.

3 Aim: to practise speaking.

● Ask the students to read out the sentences they wrote in 2. The others should guess which must be, might be and can't be true. Which pair has written the most incredible sentences?

21

GENERAL COMMENTS

Storytelling

The subject of this lesson is the story of the film *Casablanca*. A less obvious objective is to provide the students with the language to tell a story in English. Students enjoy reading and listening to stories, but they may also enjoy telling them as well. Unlike many classroom tasks, this is an activity which occurs naturally in real life, and will appeal to the students' motivation to use English in an authentic way. Perhaps the most common storytelling activity will be a simple account of a film someone has just seen, or a book someone has just read. The outcome of the activity sequence in this lesson, which you can find in *Writing and speaking* activity 2, is to provide the students with a framework for their storytelling to use on this and on other occasions. For more ideas about storytelling, see *Once Upon a Time*, by John Morgan and Mario Rinvolucri (Cambridge University Press).

Adjectives and adverbs

You may need to explain at some point in the lesson that an adjective describes a person or a thing, and an adverb describes the manner of an action.

VOCABULARY AND LISTENING

1 Aim: to present the vocabulary in the box; to prepare for listening.

● Ask the students about films which they have seen or which are popular at the moment. Ask them to look at the vocabulary box and say what type the films are.

● Ask the students if they can think of other films which you can use the words to describe. Write the suggestions on the board.

● Write on the board: *Casablanca – what type?* Ask the students if they have seen it, who were the actors, when was it made, etc.

2 Aim: to present the vocabulary in the box; to prepare for listening.

● Explain that most of the words in the box can be used to describe something in a positive or negative way. However, there will be some that, according to the context, can be both positive and negative. Write +, – and *?* on the board, and ask the students to group the words according to their meaning.

Answers

+	–	?
amazing	appalling	simple
remarkable	awkward	funny
delightful	far-fetched	emotional
charming	clumsy	extraordinary
impressive	horrible	
sensitive	terrible	
gripping	slow	
powerful		
fantastic		
spectacular		

● There may be some 'false friends' (words in English which look the same as words in another language but mean the opposite or something different). For example, in French *terrible* means *very good*, in English, *terrible* means *very bad*.

3 Aim: to practise using the words in the box.

● Ask students to match the words in activity 2 with the film titles they suggested in activity 1.

4 Aim: to listen for specific information.

● Check everyone understands the meaning of the features mentioned.

● Find out if anyone has seen *Casablanca*. Can they describe what happens?

● 🔲 Ask the students to listen and find the adjectives John uses to describe each of the features. Play the tape.

Answers
the film: brilliant, classic
the acting: fantastic, wonderful
the plot: gripping, outstanding, emotional
the ending: memorable

5 Aim: to check comprehension; to provide an opportunity for a second listening.

● Ask the students what John's favourite scene was. Do those students who have seen the film agree?

● Ask the students to work in pairs and to try and remember as much detail about the listening passage as possible.

● 🔲 Play the tape again.

GRAMMAR AND FUNCTIONS

1 Aim: to practise forming adverbs from adjectives.

● Ask the students to read the information in the grammar box and then to do the exercises.

● If your students can already form adverbs, do this activity orally with the whole class. You may want to check the spelling, so ask them to spell the adverbs.

Answers
simply, brilliantly, remarkably, delightfully, charmingly, impressively, powerfully, happily, spectacularly

2 Aim: to focus on the difference between adjectives and adverbs.

● You may need to remind the students what the difference between an adjective and an adverb is. (See introduction above.)

Answers
1 He thought it was a **spectacular** film.
2 It was **extremely** exciting.
3 The characters acted rather **clumsily.**
4 The plot was **particularly** far-fetched.
5 It's got a **fantastic** ending.
6 It's one of the most **remarkable** films I've ever seen.

SOUNDS

● 🔲 Explain that strong stress and intonation are used to emphasise an opinion. Play the tape and ask the students to listen and repeat the sentences.

WRITING AND SPEAKING

1 Aim: to focus on the position of adjectives and adverbs.

● This activity involves an awareness of word order, which is essential if writing is to be practised. There may be more than one possible position for each word, but these can be discussed later. Ask the students to do this activity alone.

● Ask the students to check their answers in pairs.

● Now check the position of the words with the whole class.

Possible answers
Casablanca is a **gripping** thriller and a **passionate** love story with Humphrey Bogart and Ingrid Bergman. The film takes place during the Second World War in Casablanca, an **exotic** city in Morocco. Rick Blaine, played by Humphrey Bogart, owns *Rick's café* which is a centre for war refugees who are waiting for visas to escape to America. Rick discovers that his former love, Ilsa Lund, played by Ingrid Bergman, is now married to a **brave** Resistance worker, Victor Laszlo, whom he is helping to escape. With the enemy on their trail, Ilsa comes to Casablanca to collect the **precious** visas which will allow Laszlo to escape and continue his fight for freedom. To her surprise she finds Rick there. Rick is still **deeply** in love with Ilsa, but he **reluctantly** decides to help the couple escape. It's full of romance, intrigue, and suspense and it's **extremely** well-filmed. My favourite scene is at the end of the film, at the airport where Rick and Ilsa **finally** have to say goodbye and she leaves with her husband on a plane just before the enemy arrives.

2 Aim: to practise telling stories.

● Ask the students to work in pairs and to talk about a film they have seen or a book they have read. As one student talks, ask the other to make notes.

3 Aim: to practise writing a story.

● Ask the students to write a paragraph about their partner's story.

● You may like to ask the students to do this activity for homework.

22

GENERAL COMMENTS

Position of adverbs

The position of adverbs and adverbial phrases is quite complex and this lesson can only raise the students' awareness of the issue. You may find it necessary to refer them to the Grammar Review or a grammar book for further explanation.

VOCABULARY AND READING

1 Aim: to present the words in the vocabulary box.

● Some students may already know some of these words, or recognise them because they look like the words in their own language. So the activity is designed to consolidate previously acquired vocabulary.
Ask them where you might find the animals mentioned. There may be more than one possible answer.

● Check that the students know what the word *extinct* means.

● Find out if the students think we should spend money on trying to preserve animals.

> **Possible answers**
> **elephant*:** Africa, India
> **tiger*:** India
> **zebra:** Africa
> **falcon:** Europe
> **wolf:** North America
> **moose:** North America
> **lion:** Africa
> **giraffe:** Africa
> **whale*:** Arctic, Antarctic
> **eagle:** North America
> **bear:** North America
> **vulture:** Africa
> **panda*:** Asia
> **leopard:** Africa
> **gorilla*:** Africa
> **rhinoceros*:** Africa
> **tortoise:** South America
> **pigeon:** Europe
> **butterfly:** Europe, Africa, North America, Asia
> **jaguar:** Africa

● Students may know that the animals marked with * have been in danger of becoming extinct.

2 Aim: to prepare for reading.

● This activity is designed to give the students an opportunity to think about the topic of the passage before they read it. Ask them to think about animals which are in danger of extinction, and to say if the situation is optimistic or pessimistic.

3 Aim: to practise reading for main ideas.

● This activity is designed to encourage the students to read for the general sense of the passage rather than for detailed comprehension.

> **Answer**
> The passage mentions the following animals: tiger, elephant, rhinoceros, whale, tortoise, pigeon, wolf, lion

4 Aim: to practise inferring.

● This activity helps the students to read between the lines.

> **Answers**
> 1 True
> 2 True
> 3 No information
> 4 True
> 5 True
> 6 True

GRAMMAR

1 Aim: to help distinguish between adverbs/adverbial phrases of time, manner, place.

● Ask the students to read the information in the grammar box and then to do the exercises.

● Your students may have noticed that it is sometimes difficult to decide if an adverb or adverbial phrase is one of time, manner or place. However, it is important that they can do this so that they know where it can go in the sentence.

> **Answers**
> 1 Twenty years ago the tiger was in trouble.= **time**
> 2 Poachers still hunt the tiger illegally. = **manner**
> 3 In Africa the most important species in danger is the elephant. = **place**
> 4 In 1979 there were 1.3 million elephants there. = **time, place**
> 5 The world agreed to ban the ivory trade completely. = **manner**
> 6 Elephant numbers in Kenya and Tanzania are increasing rapidly. = **manner**

2 Aim: to focus on the position of adverbs and adverbial phrases in a sentence.

● Explain that there may be more than one possible answer.

> **Answers**
> 1 In the past twenty years, Africa has lost 99 per cent of its black rhinos.
> 2 Ten years ago, in Kenya's Masai Mara national reserve, there were only 11 rhinos left.
> 3 The grey whales recovered quickly.
> 4 Today, there are perhaps 20,000.
> 5 Other rare species continue to receive protection all over the world.
> 6 Suddenly, wildlife is good for the tourist trade.

SPEAKING AND WRITING

1 Aim: to practise speaking.

● Ask the students to talk about the issues suggested.

● Ask one member of each group to report back on their group's views.

2 Aim: to practise writing; to practise using the linking words *X years ago, then, today,* and *in X years' time*.

● Ask the students to choose one or two of the issues they discussed in activity 1 and to write a description of how the situation has changed over the last few years. Help them to use the linking words suitably in their descriptions.

● You may like to ask the students to do this activity for homework.

23

GENERAL COMMENTS

Reported speech

This is the first of three lessons which focuses on reported speech. In this lesson the tense shift for direct to reported (or indirect) speech is presented. Reported questions are covered in Lesson 24 and reporting verbs are to be found in Lesson 25. The most common pattern is when the main verb is in the past tense and the reporting verbs remain in same the tense as they were in direct speech, for example *He said he is a doctor. She said it is raining.* Explain to the students that in a reported speech sentence it may not be necessary to retain all the words which were in the direct speech version. It is rare to find words like *yes* and *no* and question tags in reported speech. The two clauses do not always need to be separated by *that*, although this is more common in formal situations, and essential after certain verbs such as *reply.*

Punctuation

English punctuation may be different from your students' own language. You may want to explain some general rules.
- Sentences begin with a capital letter and end with a full stop, an exclamation mark or a question mark.
- You don't put question marks or exclamation marks at the beginning of sentences.
- The first person singular pronoun *I* always takes a capital letter.
- You show direct speech with inverted commas at the beginning of the statement and at the end, with the final comma, full stop or question mark, inside the inverted commas.

VOCABULARY AND READING

1 To present the topic of the lesson; to present the vocabulary in the box.

● Explain that the topic of the lesson is love and romance. Ask the students to say if the words in the box are symbols of love in their country. There are one or two strange items; this is because the symbol used in the poem they will read is also strange.

● Ask the students what the other words might symbolise in their country.

2 Aim: to prepare for reading.

● Ask the students if they know what St Valentine's Day is. What happens? What customs are there on this occasion? Does it exist in their country? If St Valentine's Day does not exist in their countries, is there anything similar?

3 Aim: to read for main ideas.

● Ask the students to read the poem for its main ideas. The task is designed to distract them from worrying too much about difficult vocabulary. However, it may be that some of the words in activity 4 are needed to help them perform this activity.

> **Answer**
> The poet is offering her lover an onion.

4 Aim: to practise using techniques for dealing with unfamiliar words.

● These words are beyond the present level of the students. However, it is useful to give the students practice in working out the meaning of difficult words from the context. It is important that they do not rely too much on you or their dictionaries.

5 Aim: to prepare for listening; to focus on the main ideas of the poem.

● Ask the students to discuss the statements and to say if they agree with them. The statements are designed to lead the students to the heart of the poem either by suggesting interpretations or by eliminating misleading suggestions.

6 Aim: to encourage students to react to the poem; to present the vocabulary in the box.

● Ask the students to find words under the headings romantic, unromantic. When they suggest a word, ask them to explain the reasons for their choice.

7 Aim: to present adjectives describing reactions.

● Ask students to look at the words in the vocabulary box and decide the poet's attitude towards her lover.

LISTENING

Aim: to practise listening for main ideas.

● 🔲 Explain that they are going to hear two people discussing the poem and reacting to the statements in *Vocabulary and reading* activity 5. Once again, there is no need for the students to attempt to understand every word. The comprehension task is simply to recognise whether they agree or disagree with the statements. Play the tape.

GRAMMAR

1 Aim: to focus on the tense shift from direct to reported speech.

● Ask the students to read the information in the grammar box and then to do the exercises.

● On this occasion, the target structures are presented primarily in the grammar box and not in the reading or listening passage. Do this activity orally with the whole class

2 Aim: to focus on the tense shift from reported speech to direct speech.

● Ask the students to read the text again and find what the poet really says.

3 Aim: to practise using reported speech.

● The practice is continued with statements which lovers might say to each other. Check everyone is also making other suitable changes to the sentences. Although attention has been given as to the time reference changes in the grammar box, it depends very much on when the statement is being reported as to the necessity for a change in time reference. For example, *She said she was going to call him this afternoon* implies the statement is being reported on the same day. You might want to point this out to your students.

4 Aim: to practise using reported speech.

● Give the students further practice in using reported speech by asking them to report on what the speakers in the *Listening* passage said about the poem. Ask them to do this activity in pairs so that they help each other remember the details of what the speakers said.

SOUNDS

1 Aim: to focus on different speaking styles.

● This activity is designed to give students the opportunity to experiment with different speaking styles. Ask them to say how the poem should sound. Demonstrate each style if necessary.

2 Aim: to focus on different speaking styles.

● 🔲 Play the poem. Ask them which style they think the speaker used. Is it the same style as they chose in activity 1?

WRITING AND SPEAKING

1 Aim: to practise speaking; to prepare for further practice of reported speech.

● Ask the students to work in small groups and to think of romantic things, people and places.

2 Aim: to practise speaking; to practise using reported speech.

● Ask each group to tell the rest of the class about the romantic things, people and places they talked about in activity 1.

3 Aim: to practise writing a poem.

● The writing practice in *Reward* Intermediate has so far been fairly controlled, in order to limit the number of mistakes. On this occasion, however, encourage the students to be as creative as they like. Their poems can be 'minimal' and simply use lists of words, or more complex, using carefully chosen sentences and even rhymes. Remind them that the poems can be about things and places as well as people.

● When they have done a first draft, suggest that they rewrite it once or twice, making improvements.

● You may like to do some or all of this activity for homework.

24

GENERAL COMMENTS

Vocabulary

The vocabulary field in this lesson is an important one. By the end of *Reward* Intermediate, the students will have covered most of the vocabulary fields which are suitable for this level, and which are suggested by the Threshold Level (see introduction for more information).

Reported questions

Although the students may not have been presented with reported questions, they will have been exposed to the principles of reported speech in the work they have done on indirect questions in Lesson 23. Once again, the main problem is that they will keep the word order of a question rather than of a statement, for example, *He asked me how was I?* instead of *He asked me how I was*.

Another important aspect of reported questions is the use of *if* and *whether*. *If* is used to report *yes/no* questions and questions without question words. *Whether* can also be used, but it is not presented in the grammar box. However, you may like to introduce it if you think your class will not be confused.

VOCABULARY

1 Aim: to present the words in the vocabulary box.

● Write the word *media* on the board and, with their books closed, ask the students to suggest as many different examples of the media as possible. Ask them to choose their favourite and least favourite medium. Which is the most effective?

● Ask the students to put the words in suitable categories of their own choice. If this activity is too free for them, suggest they put them in the three media categories, *newspaper, television, radio*. However, some students may notice that words like *independent, left wing, liberal, political* and *right wing* can go together, or *editor, reader, viewer* can also go together. Some words can go in more than one category.

2 Aim: to consolidate the acquisition of the words presented in the vocabulary box.

● Ask the students to work in pairs and to compare their categories.

3 Aim: to present the words in the vocabulary box.

● The words in this activity are often used when talking about the media. Ask the students to match the terms with the definitions.

> **Answers**
> 1 sitcom
> 2 broadsheet
> 3 tabloid
> 4 chat show
> 5 quiz show
> 6 soap opera

● You may like to explain that *sitcom* is short for *situation comedy*, and that the term *soap opera* comes from the fact that during the 1950s, special dramas were written for daytime broadcasting and were accompanied by adverts for soap powder. The terms *broadsheet* and *tabloid* originally referred to the size of paper used, but now refer to the style of newspaper and the target readers: broadsheet being more serious, and tabloids more popular.

SPEAKING AND LISTENING

1 Aim: to practise speaking.

● Ask the students to work in pairs and to discuss their reactions to the statements. Encourage a class discussion about the issues raised.

2 Aim: to practise listening for main ideas.

● 🔲 Explain that the speaker is going to talk about the media in the USA. Because the interviewer is English, the students will have the opportunity of comparing the two accents. Point out that they do not have to understand every word, only to recognise the questions the interviewer asks.

> **Answers**
> Francis asks the following questions:
> 1, 2, 5, 7, 10, 12

3 Aim: to practise speaking; to provide an opportunity for a second listening.

● Ask the students to talk about Shelley's answers to the questions. Encourage them to think of as much detail as possible.

● 🔲 Play the tape again and ask the students to check their answers.

GRAMMAR

1 Aim: to focus on the rules for reported questions.

● Ask the students to read the information in the grammar box and then to do the exercises.

● This activity is designed to help the students formulate for themselves the rules for reported questions.

> **Answers**
> 1 False
> 2 True
> 3 True
> 4 False

2 Aim: to focus on the formation of direct questions from reported questions.

● Make sure the students use punctuation suitable for questions. You may want to remind them of the rules explained in the general comments of Lesson 23.

> **Answers**
> 1 'Who are you?' she asked.
> 2 'Do you read a newspaper?' he asked.
> 3 'Why do you listen to the radio?' she asked.
> 4 'Do you watch a lot of television?' he asked.
> 5 'Have you heard the news?' she asked.
> 6 'What are you doing?' he asked.

3 Aim: to focus on the formation of reported questions.

● Do the first two questions orally with the whole class, and then ask students to complete the activity individually in writing.

> **Answer**
> 1 She asked if he read a daily newspaper.
> 2 She asked what his favourite TV programme was.
> 3 She asked if satellite television was growing.
> 4 She asked where most people listened to the radio in his country.
> 5 She asked if he read a Sunday paper.
> 6 She asked if he had watched any TV that day.

WRITING AND SPEAKING

1 Aim: to write reported questions; to prepare for writing a report of an interview.

● This activity sequence is designed to help the students write a report of an interview. Ask the students to do this activity in pairs and to write sentences reporting the questions which Francis asked Shelley.

> **Answers**
> Francis asked Shelley if people read mostly regional or national newspapers.
> Francis then asked if most people read a newspaper every day.
> Francis asked how many television channels there were.
> Francis asked what the most popular types of programmes were.
> Francis asked if radio was more or less popular than television.
> Francis asked if the government controlled the media.

2 Aim: to practise writing a report; to practise using the linking words.

● Ask the students to write Shelley's answers to Francis' questions, and to use the linking words suggested. Point out the example sentence in the Student's Book for students to use as a model.

3 Aim: to practise speaking.

● Ask the students to talk about their opinions about the media. They should ask supplementary questions and should try to remember what the people they spoke to said.

4 Aim: to practise speaking; to practise using reported speech.

● Ask the students to report back to the class what they asked people and what they answered. Make sure they use reported speech.

● You may like to ask them to write up their interviews for homework. Make sure they realise they should use reported questions and reported speech.

25

GENERAL COMMENTS

Short stories

This is the second of a series of short stories used in *Reward* Intermediate. It is difficult to find many stories which are short enough to be used in the classroom, so this, like some of the others in *Reward*, has been adapted although not necessarily simplified. The tasks which accompany the story are designed to lead the reader to the storyline and to generate the structures presented in this lesson. In real life, the student would have the opportunity to choose what he or she reads and to stop reading if he or she wasn't enjoying the story. The classroom context does not allow this kind of freedom, but the tasks which accompany the story are designed to help the students enjoy the story more rather than detract from its pleasure.

Katherine Mansfield

Katherine Mansfield was born in New Zealand in 1888. She went to London in 1908 to start her writing career. In 1909 she married and separated from her husband within a day. She spent an unhappy period in Germany, then met and married John Middleton Murry. Her brother was killed in the First World War, which turned her mind to her New Zealand childhood, which she wrote about. She developed tuberculosis in 1917 and died of its effects in 1923 in France. Her stories are mostly about events that might have happened within her own world, and describe experiences which could happen to anyone.

SPEAKING AND READING

1 Aim: to prepare for reading.

● Tell your students about Katherine Mansfield if you think this would interest them. Ask them to predict something about the story by looking at the picture and deciding where it takes place, who the people are and why it's called *A cup of tea*.

2 Aim: to prepare for reading; to predict what happens.

● Ask the students to work in pairs and to predict more about what happens. Ask them what they think the story is likely to be about. How do the sentences relate to the people in the picture?

3 Aim: to practise reading for main ideas.

● Ask the students to read the first part of the story and to check their answers to activity 1 and 2.

GRAMMAR

1 Aim: to focus on the word order in reported statements; to practise using reporting verbs.

● Ask the students to read the information in the grammar box and then to do the exercises.

● It is to be hoped that in this third lesson on reported speech that the students will be more accomplished at manipulating the structure. If they are still having difficulties, it may be useful to do the Practice Book exercises and the Resource Pack activities to give further practice. If they are happy with reported speech, ask them to do this activity orally in pairs. Explain, if necessary, that the sentences all refer to events in the story, so they can check their answers by looking at the first part again.

Answers
1 She told her to come along.
2 She told him to keep it for her.
3 She replied that she had none.
4 She asked her to give her some money.
5 She invited her home for tea.
6 She promised her she meant it.

2 Aim: to focus on the tense shift from reported to direct speech.

● Ask the students to check their answers to activity 1 by underlining the direct speech sentences.

Answers
'Come along.'
'Well, keep it for me – will you?'
'None, madam,' came the answer.
'Madam, would you let me have the price of a cup of tea?'
'Come home to tea with me.'
'I mean it,' Rosemary said smiling.

3 Aim: to prepare for activity 4.

● Remind the students that you don't always report exactly what was said in reported speech, but only the general sense. Reporting verbs are used to demonstrate the implication of what was said.

Answers
1 Rosemary, the girl
2 Rosemary, the girl
3 The girl
4 Rosemary, the girl
5 Rosemary, the girl
6 Rosemary, the girl

4 Aim: to focus on the use of reporting verbs.

● Ask the students to write down what the people actually said.

> **Possible answers**
> 1 'Please sit down,' she said.
> 2 'Don't be frightened,' she said.
> 3 'I'm sorry, I'm going to faint,' she said.
> 4 'Come and get warm,' she said.
> 5 'Don't cry,' she said.
> 6 'I'll look after you,' she said.

5 Aim: to practise using reporting verbs; to prepare for reading.

● This activity is central to the presentation of reporting verbs in this lesson, as well as giving important preparation for the reading of part two. Take plenty of time to do it. You may need to supplement it with the Resource Pack activity.

> **Answers**
> 1 She promised to arrange something.
> 2 Philip asked if he could come in.
> 3 Philip asked her to explain who the girl was.
> 4 He advised her that she was making a mistake.
> 5 She asked Philip if she was pretty.

6 Aim: to focus on the pattern of reporting verbs.

● You may want to suggest that whenever the students come across a reporting verb that they note down its pattern. Students may have used different reporting verbs in activity 5, if so, discuss their answers with the whole class.

> **Answers**
> **Activity 3**
> 1 invite 2
> 2 tell 2
> 3 say 3 (apologise is also a reporting verb but doesn't fit the patterns shown in the grammar box).
> 4 tell 2
> 5 tell 2
> 6 offer 1

READING AND VOCABULARY

1 Aim: to prepare for reading; to predict what happens.

● Ask the students to work in pairs and to predict what happens in part two of the story.

● Ask the students to tell the rest of the class what they think is going to happen.

● Ask the students to turn to Communication activity 9 on page 100 and to read part two.

2 Aim: to present the vocabulary in the box; to exploit the new words from the story; to check comprehension.

● This activity is designed to check that everyone has understood the plot of the story. First, find out if they enjoyed the story. Here are some questions you may like to ask to check comprehension.

> *What were Rosemary's motives for offering to look after the young girl?*
> *What kind of person is Rosemary/her husband?*
> *What about the girl?*
> *Which character do you have most sympathy for?*
> *Do you think the girl really insisted on leaving?*

● Lead a class discussion on the characters if your class is interested.

● Ask the students to check they remember what the words mean, and how they were used in the story. Are there any other words they would like to add to the list? Try not to explain every unfamiliar word. There are many which are not suitable for the intermediate learner.

● Ask the students to work in pairs and to use the words to reconstruct the story.

● Ask one student to start telling the story. If he/she misses out any information, another student can challenge with a question. If the first student answers correctly, he/she continues. If he/she doesn't answer correctly, the challenger takes over the telling of the story.

WRITING

Aim: to practise writing.

● Ask the students to write the story from the husband's point of view.

● You may like to ask the students to do this activity for homework.

Progress check
Lessons 21–25

GENERAL COMMENTS

You can work through this Progress check in the order shown, or concentrate on areas which may have caused difficulty in Lessons 21 to 25. You can also let the students choose the activities they would like to or feel the need to do.

VOCABULARY

1 Aim: to present phrasal verbs without objects and phrasal prepositional verbs.

● These types of multi-part verbs present fewer problems than those presented in Progress check Lessons 16 to 20. Remind the students that for every multi-part verb there is usually an equivalent verb which is more accessible for speakers of Latin-based languages, but that the multi-part verb is more common in everyday language use. Point out that many multi-part verbs can have more than one meaning.

> **Answers**
> 1 went down with
> 2 gave up
> 3 fell back on
> 4 went off
> 5 get on well with
> 6 blew up
> 7 caught up with
> 8 gave up

2 Aim: to practise using phrasal verbs without objects and phrasal prepositional verbs.

● Ask the students to use their dictionaries to find out the meanings of the other multi-part verbs and to write sentences illustrating one of the meanings.

3 Aim: to review all the vocabulary presented in Lessons 21 to 25.

● You may find that the students need more than the space available in the Practice Book. They should nevertheless use the headings to organise their vocabulary records.

GRAMMAR

1 Aim: to review the use of adjectives and adverbs.

> **Answers**
> 1 It was an **incredibly** thrilling film.
> 2 He was **amazingly** rich.
> 3 The special effects were **spectacular.**
> 4 The action was rather **slow.**
> 5 The acting was really **funny.**
> 6 It was **terribly** depressing.

2 Aim: to review the position of adverbs in sentences.

> **Possible answers**
> 1 She moved to London five years ago.
> 2 He drove slowly down the street.
> 3 One Sunday we were having lunch in a restaurant.
> 4 She works hard in the office all day.
> 5 He waited for twenty minutes at the bus stop.
> 6 Would you quickly take this letter to the post office?

3 Aim: to review the tense shift from reported to direct speech.

> **Answers**
> 1 'It's raining,' he said.
> 2 'I don't have any money,' she said.
> 3 'I like watching television,' he said.
> 4 'I'll leave early,' she said.
> 5 'I spoke to my mother last week,' he said.
> 6 'I haven't understood the question,' she said.

4 Aim: to review the tense shift from direct statements to reported speech.

> **Answers**
> 1 He said he was late.
> 2 She said she was getting angry.
> 3 He said she had gone.
> 4 She said he was working abroad.
> 5 He said he had called her that morning.
> 6 She said they would pay for that.

5 Aim: to focus on punctuation in direct speech.

6 Aim: to review the use of reported speech.

7 Aim: to review reported questions.

8 Aim: to review the use of reporting verbs.

SOUNDS

1 Aim: to focus on different ways of pronouncing the letter *e*.

● Remind the students that English vowels can be pronounced in a variety of different ways. Ask them to read the words aloud and then to group them according to the pronunciation.

● 📻 Play the tape and ask the students to repeat the words.

2 Aim: to focus on silent letters.

● Explain to the students that there are many words in English which contain letters which are not pronounced. Ask them to say the words aloud and then underline the silent consonants.

● 📻 Play the tape and ask the students to repeat the words.

3 Aim: to focus on contrastive stress.

● Remind the students that when you correct wrong information, the corrected information is stressed.

● 📻 Play the tape and ask the students to stress the correct information. There is a pause after each wrong sentence.

SPEAKING

1 Aim: to practise speaking.

● Make sure that the students work with someone they don't know very well. Ask them to talk about what they have in common.

2 Aim: to practise speaking.

● Ask students to write two sentences about themselves. They can be as inventive as they like.

3 Aim: to practise speaking.

● Ask the students to go round the class giving the information about themselves. Ask the other students to make suitable responses.

● Ask the students to write down or remember the pieces of information that other people tell them.

4 Aim: to practise speaking; to practise using reporting verbs and reported speech.

● Ask the students to find their partner again and tell each other what the other students said, and what they replied.

26

GENERAL COMMENTS

Cultural stereotypes

One of the objectives of the socio-cultural syllabus in
Reward is not just to explore, but also to challenge cultural
stereotypes, and to examine how fair they might be. This
lesson takes a look at the assumption that North American
food is all hamburgers and hot dogs, and also examines our
attitudes towards other culinary traditions, including that
of the students' own culture.

Topics

During the research for *Reward*, about a hundred teaching
institutions around the world responded to a
questionnaire, in which they were asked questions about
the topics which were likely to motivate the students. At
the top of the list of motivating topics were travel, and then
food and drink. The topic of this lesson is designed to
appeal directly to most students' interests and to deal with
a subject which they would discuss both inside and outside
the classroom.

VOCABULARY AND SPEAKING

**1 Aim: to present the vocabulary in the box;
to pre-teach some items used in the
reading passage.**

● Before you begin the lesson material, ask your
students to suggest any food which they particularly like
or dislike. Do they enjoy *fast food* such as hamburgers?
Or do they prefer long, elaborate meals, or something in
between? What do they usually eat at breakfast, lunch
and dinner? Write the words on the board.

● Ask the students to look at the words in the box.
Spend time with the class checking that everyone
understands what the words mean. Encourage other
students to explain the meaning to anyone for whom a
word is unfamiliar.

● Ask the students to work in groups of two or three
and to categorise words under the headings.
Remind them that some words can go under more
than one heading.

Answers

ways of preparing food: chop, cut, mix, peel,
pour, slice, spread
ways of cooking: bake, boil, casserole, cook, fry,
grill, heat, roast
food: avocado, beans, cream, green peppers, ham,
hamburger, hot dog, mussels, oil, onion, oysters,
pasta, pepper, pie, pizza, roast, salt, seafood,
spread, turkey
kitchen equipment: bowl, casserole, dish, fork,
frying pan, grill, knife, oven, plate, saucepan,
spoon

In US English, *green peppers* are also called *bell
peppers. To casserole* (verb) something is a way of
cooking slowly in a sauce, where *a casserole* (noun)
is the dish itself. Similarly, *a roast* is any large piece
of meat which has been roasted, or a way of cooking
if used as a verb. A *spread* is something you spread
on bread. *Slice* and *peel* can be both nouns and
verbs.

**2 Aim: to practise using the vocabulary presented in
the box; to practise speaking.**

● Ask the students to talk about typical food, and ways
of preparing and cooking food in their countries. If your
students are from the same country and culture, which
is the most typical food?

3 Aim: to prepare for reading; to practise speaking.

● Ask the students to talk about their impression of
typical North American food. Write up the words they
suggest on the board. Do they have a positive or a
negative impression?

READING AND LISTENING

1 Aim: to practise reading for main ideas; to react to a text.

● Ask the students to read the text about cooking in the USA, and ask them to decide which food they would like to try. There should be few vocabulary difficulties, so ask other students to explain the meaning of any unfamiliar words.

● Ask the students to talk about their impression of North American cooking. If your students come from a country which is proud of its cooking tradition, they may still remain unimpressed by the diversity and appeal of North American food. Ask them to compare its qualities with North American food, and to contrast its basic ingredients and approaches to cooking.

2 Aim: to practise listening for specific information.

● 🔲 Explain that you are going to play a tape in which a North American chef talks more about North American cooking. Ask the students to listen and to find out where the dishes come from. If your students need help, write on the board, *New York, West Coast, Texas, New England, Deep South, North-West.* There is one extra dish, hashed browns, from New York which will be described in activity 4.

> **Answers**
> **scrapple:** from New England
> **grand central oyster stew:** from New York
> **jambalaya:** from the Deep South
> **tacos:** from Texas/Mexico (Tex Mex)
> **cioppino:** from the West Coast

● Don't correct this activity yet, as students will do this in pairs in *Grammar* activity 1.

3 Aim: to check listening comprehension.

● Ask the students to try and remember the dishes the chef mentioned. Match the dishes to the ingredients.

> **Answers**
> 1 jambalaya 2 tacos 3 scrapple 4 cioppino
> 5 grand central oyster stew
>
> The extra dish is hashed browns.

● 🔲 Ask the students to check their answers in pairs. Then play the tape again.

4 Aim: to present the target structure; to practise listening for text organisation.

● Ask the students to read the instructions for the recipe and to put them in the right order.

● Play the tape and ask them to listen and check.

> **Answers**
> c e d b a

● Find out if anyone would like to taste hashed browns.

FUNCTIONS

1 Aim: to practise asking and saying what dishes are.

● Ask the students to read the information in the grammar box and then do the exercises.

● Ask the students to work in pairs and to check their answers to *Reading and listening* activity 2.

2 Aim: to practise giving instructions.

● Even students who are not interested in cooking should know how to prepare very simple food and drink. Elicit instructions as to how to make one of the food items with the whole class, then ask the students to write instructions for the rest on their own.

3 Aim: to practise giving special advice.

● You may want to play the tape again for this activity, to remind the students about the chef's special advice.

● Ask the students to work in pairs and to check the special advice the chef gives.

4 Aim: to practise giving special advice.

● Most students will have different ways of preparing food or drink, but in case most of them don't, do this activity with the whole class. Does anyone suggest any really useful advice?

SPEAKING

1 Aim: to practise speaking; to revise the vocabulary of food and drink.

● Ask the students to think about the food from their own country and to think of basic ingredients. For example, do they use oil or butter? Does every meal have meat? Is milk or rice a basic ingredient?

2 Aim: to practise speaking; to practise using the vocabulary of food and drink.

● Ask the students to work in pairs and to discuss their lists.

● Try and establish a list of basic ingredients that everyone in your class, wherever they come from, will agree on.

3 Aim: to practise speaking; to practise using the vocabulary of food and drink.

● Finish the lesson with a general discussion about typical dishes, favourite food and drink. What are the most popular dishes in your class?

● For homework, you may like to ask students to write a recipe for a dish they like.

27
GENERAL COMMENTS

Defining relative clauses

Your students may have come across defining or identifying relative clauses before. In *Reward* Pre-intermediate, *who* and *which* were presented, and elsewhere there have been numerous examples of the structure. The most common type of mistake is where the student repeats the personal pronoun in the relative clause, for example, *He's the man who he does the cooking at the hotel*, or uses the wrong relative pronoun, for example, *There's a swimming pool who belongs to the house*. If anyone uses *whom*, you may like to explain that this object pronoun is uncommon in spoken English. *That* often replaces *who* and *which* in defining relative clauses, and is particularly common after *all, every(thing), some(thing) any(thing), no(thing) none, little, few, much* and *only*, and superlatives. Prepositions can come either before the relative pronoun or at the end of the clause. *The people with whom we're staying* or *The people who we're staying with*. In spoken English, the latter is more common.

SPEAKING AND VOCABULARY

1 Aim: to introduce the theme of the lesson; to practise speaking.

● Before the students open their books, ask them to suggest different ways of communicating with people. Write their suggestions on the board.

● When someone suggests *postcards* ask the students to think about when they send postcards and to whom. Have they always sent postcards? If no one ever sends postcards, pass onto activity 2. Ask the students to talk about what they write on their postcards or letters to friends in general.

2 Aim: to present the vocabulary in the box; to practise speaking.

● Ask the students to underline words in the box which they associate with a good holiday. Can they use them to describe any holidays they've had? Ask them to compare their answers with another student.

READING

1 Aim: to practise reading for main ideas.

● Explain that the postcards are typical of what British people write and send to friends when they're away. The picture on the postcard in each case represents a summary of part of what the writers describe. Ask them to match the picture with the message.

Answers
Postcard with reference to Tokyo - top left-hand picture.
Postcard with reference to the quiet village/interior designers - top right-hand picture.
Postcard with reference to the hotel overlooking the sea - bottom picture.

2 Aim: to focus on linking ideas; to prepare for practice of the target structures.

● Write the underlined words on the board and ask the students to decide what they refer to. This will help them perform *Grammar* activity 4.

Answers
1 The village in the photo.
2 The house.
3 Their holiday.
4 In the hotel in the hills.
5 In the other cities.
6 The cities.

GRAMMAR

1 Aim: to link sentences using relative clauses.
- Ask the students to read the information in the grammar box and then to do the exercises.

- Ask the students to do this activity on their own, and then to check their answers with another student.

Answers
1 This is my friend **whose** house is for sale.
2 I spent two years in France **where** I learnt to speak French.
3 We went away with some friends **who** I work with.
4 I lost the photos **which** I took on holiday.
5 My sister **whose** company makes computers works in Italy.
6 Why not spend a holiday in Recife **where** it's nice and warm?

2 Aim: to focus on leaving out the relative pronoun.
- Remind the students that you can only leave *who* or *which*.

Answer
You can only leave out *which* in 4.

3 Aim: to focus on inserting the relative pronoun.
- Ask the students to read the postcards again and to decide where they could insert *who* or *which*.

Answers
It's probably the most beautiful place **which** we've ever seen, and very quiet.
The nicest person **who** we've met is Spiros ...
The town **which** I liked best was ...

SOUNDS

1 Aim: to focus on pauses in defining and non-defining relative clauses.
- You may like to explain to the students that a comma in written English roughly corresponds to a pause in spoken English. It is very usual to pause at the beginning of a non-defining relative clause, which is separated from the main clause by a comma. (You also pause at the end if the clause is set in the middle of a sentence.) Because a defining relative clause is part of the main clause and has no comma, it isn't usual to pause.

Answers
This year, I'm spending my summer vacation, which is six weeks long, in a small village near the Lakes, which is very relaxing. The place where I'm staying only has about a hundred people, who are mostly farmers, although it gets crowded in summer when the people from Milan, who have second homes in the region, come and spend their holidays here too.

2 Aim: to focus on pauses in defining and non-defining relative clauses.
- ▣ Play the tape and ask the students to listen and check they have put commas where the speaker pauses.

LISTENING AND WRITING

1 Aim: to prepare for listening.
- Ask the students to look at the questions and to think about their answers. They can talk about their answers in pairs or groups of three.

2 Aim: to practise listening for main ideas.
- ▣ Ask the students to listen and decide which questions the speakers are answering.

Answers
1 Where is the most beautiful place you've ever been on holiday?
2 What is the most frightening thing that has ever happened to you on holiday?
3 What is the most exciting thing you've ever done on holiday?

3 Aim: to check listening comprehension; to provide an opportunity for a second listening.
- ▣ Ask the students to check how much they remember and understood about the people speaking in activity 2. Play the tape again.

4 Aim: to practise writing.
- Ask the students to choose one of the questions in *Listening and writing* activity 1 and to write a postcard describing the person, place or experience they've just had, with as much detail as possible. The length of the writing depends on how much they can fit onto a postcard (within reason, of course!).

- You may like to ask them to do this activity for homework.

28

GENERAL COMMENTS

Target and sample cultures

In this lesson the students read about British produce that is part of British culture. This provides an opportunity for cross-cultural comparison and discussion.

The passive

Students often have difficulty with active and passive forms. A typical mistake is *I'm boring* instead of *I'm bored*. Most students will have seen the passive in some form, although in *Reward* Pre-intermediate, the students will only have seen the present passive. You may want to support the work on the passive with a Resource Pack activity.

VOCABULARY AND READING

1 Aim: to present the vocabulary in the box; to pre-teach some unfamiliar words; to prepare for reading.
● Many of the words in the box will appear in the reading passage, so care taken at this stage to explain and pre-teach unfamiliar items will allow for some fluent reading practise.

● Ask the students to underline the verbs.

● Ask the students to say the verbs aloud, and write them on the board.

● Ask the students to work in groups of three or four, and to write the nouns. Make sure they think about the *person* as well as the *thing*.

● Ask each group to call out a noun in turn. Give a mark for each correct answer.

Answers

verbs	nouns
build	building, builder
design	design, designer
grow	growth, grower
invent	invention, inventor
make	make, maker
manufacture	manufacture, manufacturer
mine	mine, miner
produce	produce, product, producer

2 Aim: to consolidate and expand the new vocabulary.
● Ask the students to match the verbs with suitable nouns from the box.

Answers
build: cars, computers, factory, ships, power station, workshop
design: cars, computers, pottery, ships, power station, workshop
grow: bananas, coffee, cotton, fruit, rice, tobacco, wool
make: beer, cars, china, computers, electricity, iron, pottery, ships, tea, wine
manufacture: beer, cars, china, cloth, computers, cotton, pottery, ships, wine, wool
mine: coal, gold, iron
produce: beer, cars, china, cloth, computers, cotton, electricity, pottery, rice, ships, steel, tea, tobacco, wheat, wine, wool

Only *grow* refers to a natural process.

3 Aim: to practise reading for main ideas and for specific information.
● Ask the students to look at the map of Britain. What products do they think the drawings symbolise?

● Ask the students to read the passage and to decide if Britain has more natural produce or manufactured produce.

Answers
natural produce: whisky, pottery, coal, cider, wool
manufactured produce: shipbuilding, steel

4 Aim: to practise dealing with unfamiliar words
● The techniques suggested are ones which can be used with any unfamiliar words. It's important for the students to develop these word skills which will help them avoid trying to understand every single word and encourage them to achieve fluency in reading.

● Ask the students to compare their answers in pairs.

Answers
nouns: clay, cutlery, iron ore, mill, stream, distillery, cider, orchard
verbs: bred, mill, stream
manufactured product: cutlery
natural product: clay, cider,
place: mill, distillery, orchard

5 Aim: to encourage cross-cultural comparison.
● This activity is designed to list Britain's produce and to compare with the produce from the students' own country or countries.

GRAMMAR

1 Aim: to focus on the form of passive tenses.

● Ask the students to read the information in the grammar box and then to do the exercises.

● This is an inductive activity designed to focus on the different forms of the passive. There should be at least one example of every passive mentioned.

> **Answers**
> **Scotland:** is thought (present)
>   are often situated (present)
>   will be encouraged (future)
> **Staffordshire:** is made (present)
>   is collected (present) were built (past)
>   were brought (past) was exported (past)
> **South Wales:** was still mined (past)
>   was being affected (past continuous)
>   was stopped (past)
> **Hereford:** are brought...processed...distributed
>   (present)
> **Glasgow:** was known (past)
>   was widened (past) could be built (modal)
>   has been affected (present perfect)
>   is being reduced (present continuous)
> **Yorkshire:** have been bred (present perfect)
> **Sheffield:** were first manufactured (past)
>   are needed (present)

2 Aim: to practise using passive tenses.

● You may like to do this activity orally with the whole class.

> **Answers**
> 1 Gunpowder **was discovered** in China.
> 2 Scotch whisky **is exported** all over the world.
> 3 Today, shipbuilding **is being affected** by competition from the Far East.
> 4 Wine **has been made** in France for centuries.
> 5 In the next century, more whisky **will be exported** from Scotland than wine from France.

3 Aim: to practise using the passive.

● Ask the students to rewrite the sentences in the passive. You may like to discuss with them whether the sentences are better in the active or the passive. Remind them that this will depend on what they consider to be the most important information.

> **Answers**
> 1 Three times as many bicycles **are made** in China as in the USA and Japan.
> 2 More money **is earned** in a year by Exxon, a giant oil company in New York, than by many countries.
> 3 Coal **was** first **mined** by the Romans in the first century AD.
> 4 3,000 million flowers a year **are grown** by the Dutch.
> 5 Twice as much fuel **is used** by the average American as by the average European.

4 Aim: to decide if a sentence is more effective in the active or the passive.

● This activity will be largely a matter of opinion and an appreciation of opinion, but answers are included as a rough guide.

> **Possible answers**
> 1 b The important information is the land; it's obvious who uses it.
> 2 a The focus is on the Japanese here and what they like, rather than the fish which is eaten.
> 3 a We're more interested in who used tobacco as a flower, rather than what was done to it.

SPEAKING AND WRITING

1 Aim: to practise speaking; to prepare for writing; to practise using the passive.

● Ask the students to think about produce from their region or country. Find out if it is something they are particularly proud of. Is it better from this country or region than from anywhere else? Take the opportunity to challenge assumptions about certain countries being known for producing the best commodities, for example, French wine, Italian shoes, German cars.

● Ask students to continue the discussion with their partner, using the prompts in the student's book to help them.

2 Aim: to practise speaking; to prepare for writing; to practise using the passive.

● Ask the students to go round asking and talking about their local products. They should take notes.

3 Aim: to practise writing; to practise using the passive.

● Ask the students to write up their notes about the products mentioned by different people.

● You may like to ask the students to do this activity for homework.

29

GENERAL COMMENTS

Vocabulary and reading

At this stage in *Reward*, the students will be more autonomous in their reading skills. A number of different microskills have already been practised: reading for main ideas, reading for specific purposes, dealing with unfamiliar words, evaluating the text, inferring, understanding text organisation. The vocabulary work accompanying the reading texts has one or more of the following purposes: to focus on the vocabulary which is suitable to be acquired at this level and at this stage of the course; to pre-teach difficult items; to help the students have access to the main ideas of a text; to encourage the students to develop effective ways of dealing with unfamiliar vocabulary. In the last case it isn't important for the student to record the vocabulary items in question; they are simply obstacles to overcome in order to understand the general sense of the passage.

Cross-cultural awareness

The passage comes from the diary of someone looking for somewhere to live. You may wish to discuss with your students if they are generally happy with where they live or if they would prefer to choose somewhere else.

VOCABULARY AND READING

1 Aim: to present the vocabulary in the box; to pre-teach some unfamiliar words.

● Ask the students to tell the class what features and amenities their ideal home would have. Write them on the board. Where would it be? How many rooms would it have? What size would it be? Would it be old or modern? What kind of view would it have?

● Ask the students to work in pairs, look at the list of words and explain to each other the meaning of difficult words.

● Ask the students to match the adjectives in the first box with the nouns in the second box.

Possible answers
blocked: tap, shower, toilet, sink, bath
torn: carpet, armchair, sofa, curtains, wallpaper
worn: carpet, armchair, sofa
faded: wallpaper, curtains, carpet
dirty: toilet, sink, bath, oven, shutters, window pane
broken: tap, shower, toilet, dishwasher, armchair, sofa, stairs
dusty: carpet, armchair, sofa, table, curtains, shutters, window pane
not working: tap, shower, oven, toilet, light, dishwasher, sink, bath, lawnmower, wiring
overgrown: garden
overflowing: toilet, sink, bath
dripping: tap, bath, sink, shower
stuck: tap, shutters, gate, window pane
scratched: table
stained: toilet, sink, bath, oven, table, ceiling, wall
old-fashioned: armchair, sofa, shower, toilet, sink, bath
peeling: shutters, walls

2 Aim: to present the vocabulary in the box; to pre-teach some unfamiliar words.

● Ask the students to continue the collocation activities by matching the jobs with the words in activity 1.

Answers
builder: ceiling, wall, stairs
carpenter: table, gate, stairs
clean: tap, shower, oven, carpet, toilet, armchair, sofa, table, curtains, light, dishwasher, stairs, sink, bath, shutters, wallpaper, wall, window pane
cut: lawnmower
decorator: ceiling, wall, stairs, wallpaper
electrician: light, wiring
gardener: garden, lawnmower
fix: tap, shower, oven, toilet, armchair, table, curtains, light, dishwasher, gate, sink, bath, lawnmower, shutters
mend: tap, shower, oven, toilet, armchair, table, curtains, light, dishwasher, gate, sink, bath, lawnmower, shutters, wiring
paint: table, gate, stairs, shutters, ceiling, wall
plumber: tap, shower, toilet, dishwasher, sink
repair: armchair, table, dishwasher, gate, sink, bath, lawnmower, shutters, wiring
replaster: wall, ceiling
replace: tap, shower, oven, toilet, armchair, table, curtains, light, dishwasher, gate, sink, bath, lawnmower, shutters, wiring
wash: carpet, curtains, shutters, ceiling, wall

3 Aim: to practise reading for main ideas.

● There should be few vocabulary problems which have not been covered in the pre-teaching phases, so restrict the use of dictionaries while your students read this text. Ask them to decide where the text comes in the man's search.

> **Answer**
> From the beginning.

4 Aim: to practise dealing with unfamiliar words.

● Remember that the aim of focusing on these words is not for them to be learnt and recorded but so that they do not distract the reader from the general sense of the passage. They contribute colour and depth to the text's style, not essential meaning.

> **Answers**
> **battered:** broken
> **in shreds:** torn
> **dense:** overgrown
> **antiquated:** old-fashioned
> **filthy:** dirty

5 Aim: to provide an opportunity for a second reading; to prepare for the presentation of the target structures.

● Ask the students to note down everything that is wrong with the house. Their answers will be used in *Grammar* activity 1.

> **Answers**
> basin – filthy, bedroom – dusty, gate – broken, grass – overgrown, garden path – dusty, house – dusty, light – not working, shutters – peeling, sofa – faded, armchairs – battered, curtains – in shreds, undergrowth – dense, water – to be reconnected

GRAMMAR

1 Aim: to practise using *need* + *-ing* and passive infinitive.

● Ask the students to read the information in the grammar box and then to do the exercises.

● Ask the students to write sentences saying what needs to be done to the house in the passage. Encourage them to use both constructions in turn.

> **Answers**
> The gate needs to be mended.
> The grass needs cutting.
> The garden path needs sweeping.
> The house needs to be cleaned.
> The light needs mending.
> The shutters need to be repainted.
> The armchairs need replacing.

> The curtains need to be mended.
> The undergrowth needs cutting.
> The water needs to be reconnected.
> The basin needs cleaning.

2 Aim: to practise using causative constructions with *have* and *get*.

● Tell the students that they can use some of the jobs in the vocabulary box in *Vocabulary and listening* activity 2 to say who you ask to do the things.

> **Possible answers**
> 1 I'll get a carpenter to mend the gate.
> 2 I'll have a gardener to cut the grass.
> 3 I'll get a cleaner to clean the house.
> 4 I'll get an electrician to reconnect the electricity.
> 5 I'll have a decorator paint the shutters.
> 6 I'll have a plumber to reconnect the water.

3 Aim: to focus on reflexive pronouns.

● Since the main point of causative constructions is the idea of having something done by somebody else, this is a suitable moment to introduce reflexive pronouns and to focus on what you would do yourself.

● Do this activity with the whole class, then individually in writing. Who is the most competent or versatile at do-it-yourself in the class?

SPEAKING

1 Aim: to practise speaking; to review the vocabulary presented in this lesson.

● Ask the students to think about the state of their homes. Explain that someone who is houseproud is someone who likes their home to be clean, tidy and well-decorated. What would you see if you visited their homes right now? Ask them to describe the scene. Find out who is houseproud and who doesn't care.

● Ask the students to say what's wrong or what needs doing in their homes at the moment.

2 Aim: to practise speaking; to review the vocabulary presented in this lesson; to practise using reflexive pronouns.

● Ask the students to go round the class describing what needs to be done in their homes at the moment. Find out who is going to do it.

● You may like to ask students to write up a survey for homework.

3 Aim: to practise speaking; to review the vocabulary presented in this lesson.

● Ask the students to work in groups and to design a home which would suit them all. Explain that they all have to live under the same roof, so that if anyone needs privacy, this has to be taken into consideration. Ask them also to think about rooms, furniture, fittings and location. They will have done some of the preparatory work for this at the beginning of the lesson.

30

GENERAL COMMENTS

Sport

One of the most popular topics, and one of the most common situations in which the students will be confronted with English, is sport, especially on an international level. But, like pop music and fashion, sport cannot always be successfully treated in textbooks, as it is only of interest in a very contemporary context. However, the textbook can create the context in which the topic can be discussed, perhaps as an addition to more up-to-date material which the teacher has prepared for the class.

Verb patterns: *make* and *let,* infinitive constructions after adjectives

The most common mistake with *make* + object + verb is to include *to* with the infinitive, for example, *Make them to play with heavier rackets.* This is also a common mistake with *let,* as well as using the *-ing* form or the past simple of the verb which follows, for example, *I would let the referee looking at a video recording. He let me left the pitch early.* It may be useful to write up some of the target structures on the board at the start of the lesson, so that you can point them out if a student makes a mistake.

VOCABULARY

1 Aim: to present the vocabulary in the box; to pre-teach some unfamiliar words.

● Write on the board a series of ages: 5 years, 15 years, 25 years, 45 years, 65 years. Ask the students to say what sports people do at these ages.

● Ask the students to look at the vocabulary box. Your students will be acquainted with many of these words, since they will have become part of their lexicon without ever having been taught! Which words are the same as or similar to words in their own language?

● Ask the students to say which words are sports.

> **Answers**
> basketball, boxing, swimming, skiing, football, tennis, athletics

● This is a good opportunity to review or present other sporting vocabulary. Ask students to suggest types of sport, where it's played, who plays it, what equipment is used and how, if at all, it's scored.

2 Aim: to practise using the words in the box; to focus on collocation.

● Ask the students to group the other words with the sports.

> **Answers**
> **basketball:** basket, compete, referee, player, court, game, run, score, send off
> **boxing :** compete, referee, ring, fight, boots, match, boxer, score
> **swimming:** compete, referee, pool, race, score, lane
> **skiing:** compete, referee, slope, boots, run, score, race
> **football:** compete, goal, play, referee, player, field, boots, match, game, run, score, send off
> **tennis:** compete, play, serve, player, court, racket, match, game
> **athletics:** athlete, compete, field, match, run, score, race, lane

● Ask the students to add to their lists any words they thought of in activity 1.

READING AND LISTENING

1 Aim: to prepare for reading and listening.

● Introduce the reading task by asking students which sports they enjoy. Find out if there are any they don't enjoy. If not, why? Can their favourite sports be improved?

2 Aim: to practise reading for main ideas.
- Ask the students to read the text and decide which sports the suggestions refer to.

Answers
1 swimming 2 football 3 basketball 4 boxing
5 tennis 6 skiing 7 football 8 tennis

3 Aim: to practise listening for main ideas.
- 📼 Play the tape and ask the students to check their answers to activity 1.

4 Aim: to present the target structures; to check listening comprehension; to provide an opportunity for a second listening.
- Ask the students to work in pairs and to try and remember as much about the listening passage as possible. Go round the class and check what they remember.

- Now ask them to match the suggestions in activity 1 with the statements.

Answers
1 d 2 h 3 a 4 g 5 f 6 e 7 b 8 c

- 📼 Play the tape again for the students to check their answers.

GRAMMAR

1 Aim: to practise using *make, let* or *not let*.
- Ask the students to read the information in the grammar box and then to do the exercises.

- Check that the students can manipulate this structure by asking them to complete the sentences. You can do this activity orally.

Answers
1 Would you **let** me take you to the match?
2 They **don't let** you touch the ball in football.
3 They **let** you have two serves in tennis.
4 They **made** him swim in a freezing pool.
5 They **make** you stay in your seats in stadiums in Britain.
6 Do they **let** you touch the ball with your head?

2 Aim: to practise using *make* and *let*.
- Ask the students to work in pairs and to talk about their reactions to the suggestions made in the reading and listening passages.

- Ask the students to choose a sport and to make a few changes to the rules. They can be as inventive or as unreasonable as they like!

3 Aim: to practise using adjective + infinitives.
- Ask the students to do this activity alone, then to check their answers with a partner.

Answers
1 Football is very exciting to watch.
2 It's essential to slow the game down.
3 It's sometimes difficult to get tickets.
4 It's unusual for girls to play football.
5 It's getting very easy to score goals.
6 It's good for children to be interested in sport.
7 It's pleasant to play tennis.
8 It's expensive to do sport professionally.

SOUNDS

Aim: to focus on stressed words in sentences.
- Remind the students that a speaker is likely to stress the words which he/she considers to be important. Ask them to underline the important words.

- 📼 Play the tape and ask the students to check the words which the speaker stresses. Are they the words they've underlined?

Answers
<u>I</u> would make them use a <u>circular</u> pool and make them try to <u>pass</u> each other, so that it's more like a <u>running</u> race. It would be <u>easier</u> to see that they're <u>competing</u> against each other.

<u>I</u> would let the <u>referee</u> look at a <u>video</u> recording before he <u>decides</u> to send a player <u>off</u>. It's very <u>hard</u> to make up your <u>mind</u> if you haven't seen <u>exactly</u> what <u>happened</u>.

SPEAKING

1 Aim: to practise speaking; to practise using the target structures.
- This is the stage of the lesson in which the students are encouraged to talk as much as they like about sport. You may like to introduce some topical sporting references at this stage, and to ask students which teams they support, how these teams are doing and what their future is likely to be this season.

- Ask the students to read the statements and to decide if they agree with them.

- Ask the students if they like sport and if so, why.

2 Aim: to practise speaking; to practise using the target structures.
- Ask the students to do a review of the class's reactions to the statements.

- For homework, you may like to ask them to write about the class reactions.

Progress check Lessons 26–30

GENERAL COMMENTS

You can work through this Progress check in the order shown, or concentrate on areas which may have caused difficulty in Lessons 26 to 30. You can also let the students choose the activities they would like to or feel the need to do.

VOCABULARY

1 Aim: to present common verb + noun combinations.
● Explain to the students that, like multi-part verbs, verb + noun combinations are commonly used in English and, if used correctly, give the impression of fluency. Encourage them to record these combinations as single vocabulary items under suitable headings in their *Wordbanks*.

> **Answers**
> **have:** an opinion, time, help, visitors, a lecture, a cold, a party, room, a point, a test
> **take:** time, prisoners, a taxi, a note, a test, advice
> **do:** your hair, your best, the ironing, the washing, damage
> **make:** time, a mistake, the bed, room, a move, a note, a point, an example
> **give:** an opinion, time, your best, a lecture, a party, advice, a smile

2 Aim: to practise common verb + noun combinations.

> **Answers**
> 1 make 2 done 3 taking 4 take 5 having

3 Aim: to focus on words which are often confused.
● This activity focuses on words which look similar in English but don't have the same meaning. Suggest to your students that they write down the two confusable words together, so that they will be easier to revise.

4 Aim: to practise using words which are often confused.

> **Answers**
> 1 The government revealed its new **economic** strategy.
> 2 He was very **sensitive** to criticism.
> 3 Can I **lend** you some money?
> 4 Can I **check** your ticket to see if you've got the right one?
> 5 I **lay** down on the bed.

● Spend time exploring the meaning of the other words. Ask the students to write sentences illustrating the different meanings.

5 Aim: further practice in the use of words which are often confused.

> **Answers**
> 1 I was **watching** television when I **heard** a noise outside.
> 2 When you **lose** weight, your trousers are **loose**.
> 3 When you come to our party, **take** a taxi and **bring** a bottle.
> 4 I'm **waiting** for a bus. I'm **expecting** one any minute now.
> 5 **Actually**, I want to come and see you right **now**.

6 Aim: to review vocabulary present in Lessons 26 to 30.
● Encourage the students to add words to their *Wordbanks*.

GRAMMAR

1 Aim: to review the use of imperatives and *always, never, make sure you, don't forget to.*
● Encourage the students to write their instructions and then to show them to other students.

2 Aim: to revise defining relative clauses.

> **Answers**
> 1 This is the car **which** is for sale.
> 2 She went to the USA **where** she met her husband.
> 3 On holiday he met a friend **who** he knew from home.
> 4 Someone stole the bag **which** she bought in Paris.
> 5 She lives with a friend **whose** family owns a large house in the country.

3 Aim: to revise the omission of the relative pronoun.

> **Answers**
> 3 4

4 Aim: to review the form and use of the passive.

> **Answers**
> 1 Mercedes cars **are made** in Germany.
> 2 Skiing **was invented** in Norway.
> 3 Champagne **has been produced** in France for centuries.
> 4 In the future more ships **will be built** in the Far East than in Europe.
> 5 It **is recognised** that smoking is bad for your health.

5 Aim: to review *need + -ing* or *need + to be done*.

● Encourage the students to alternate between the two structures.

> **Answers**
> 1 It needs taking to the garage.
> 2 It needs to be mended.
> 3 The house needs redecorating.
> 4 It needs to be cut.
> 5 It needs reconnecting.

6 Aim: to review the use of reflexive pronouns.

● Ask the students to write sentences saying which of the jobs in activity 5 they will do themselves and which they will get someone to do.

7 Aim: to review *make, let* and *don't let +* object + infinitive.

> **Answers**
> 1 They **make** him arrive at eight-thirty.
> 2 They **don't let** him go home for lunch.
> 3 They **let** him go home at four in the afternoon.
> 4 They **make** him work on Saturdays.
> 5 They **let** him have six weeks holiday.

SOUNDS

1 Aim: to focus on the different ways of pronouncing the letter *i*.

● Ask the students to say the words aloud.

● Then ask the students to put the words in groups according to the pronunciation of the letter *i*.

> **Answers**
> /aɪ/: bite knife pie iron rice light
> /ɪ/: bit dish pick olive

● 📼 Play the tape and ask the students to repeat the words.

2 Aim: to focus on /ʃ/ and /dʒ/.

● Write the words on the board and underline the sounds this activity focuses on.

● Then ask the students to put the words in two groups.

> **Answers**
> /ʃ/: precious finish shower share suspicious
> /dʒ/: stranger change passenger suggest
>   danger job

● 📼 Play the tape and ask the students to check their groups of words and repeat them.

3 Aim: to focus on /eə/, /aɪ/ and /eɪ/.

● Ask the students to match the words with the sounds.

> **Answers**
> 1 /haɪ/high   2 /waɪ/why   3 /weər/wear
> 4 /heɪ/ hay   5 /beər/ bear   6 /baɪ/buy
> 7 /beɪ/ bay   8 /heər/ hair   9 /deɪ/ day
> 10 /weɪ/ way   11 /deər/ dare   12 /daɪ/ die

● 📼 Play the tape and ask the students to repeat the words.

READING AND WRITING

1 Aim: to practise understanding text organisation.

● Ask the students to decide where the sentences can go.

> **Answers**
> 1 The first car was invented by Nicholas Cugnot in France. **It was powered by steam and looked like a giant kettle.** On its trial-run it ran perfectly for the first few minutes. But when Cugnot increased the speed, he lost control and crashed into a wall.
> 2 People and horses in England were frightened by the motor car when it was first introduced. It was considered to be noisy, dangerous and dirty. **Speed checks were set up in 1902.** Policemen hid behind hedges to catch drivers who were going too fast.
> 3 When the first escalator was installed in Harrods, the department store in London, the ride was considered to be dangerous by some people. So the management decided to serve brandy free of charge to any passengers who felt faint when they reached the top. **It is reported that a stream of customers began to use the machine again and again, feeling faint each time!** It soon became a success.

2 Aim: to focus on word order in sentences.

● This activity focuses on word order, which is a skill which needs special attention if the students are going to write accurate English. Ask them to think of words which can go into the passage; suggest that the easiest words will be adjectives and adverbs. Ask them to write them on a separate piece of paper.

3 Aim: to focus on word order in sentences.

● Ask the students to exchange their words. They should decide where their partner's words can go in the passage.

● You can turn this into a competition: Student A must try to find a word which can only go in one position; if Student B can only find one position, Student A gets a point; if Student B can find more than one possible position, he gets the point. Change round each time.

31

GENERAL COMMENTS

If and *in case*

Students may confuse *if* and *in case*. A common mistake would be *Come and see us in case you're in town.* The explanation in the grammar box is succinct because of restrictions of space, so you may like to suggest that the students look at the explanation in the Grammar Review at the back of the book to consolidate the use of the structure. Students may also have come across it in phrases such as *in case of fire* where its meaning is much closer to *if*.

Cross-cultural training in the classroom

It may be that personal questions about belongings may not be appropriate to your students. With the development of humanistic and holistic teaching methodology, textbook writers and teachers may sometimes transgress the usual boundary of acceptable behaviour in the interests of creating a meaningful learning context. Questions such as *What's your first name?* or *What did you do at the weekend?* and activities such as *Turn out your pockets and describe the objects you find* or *Describe the worst day of your life* may be intended to give the students something universal to talk about but may not be suitable within a given cultural context. A teacher once said, 'If I asked my dinner guests to do what I ask my students to do in class, they would never return my invitation.' This kind of inappropriate behaviour is a risk that textbooks and teachers who are insensitive to the cultural context of the students are confronted with. You may therefore decide that the first activity is not a suitable one for your class.

VOCABULARY AND LISTENING

1 **Aim: to present the vocabulary in the box; to introduce the theme of the lesson.**
● Ask the students to stand back-to-back. Give Student A an object, such as a watch, a credit card, a wallet/purse. Student B must try and discover what the object is that Student A has been given. Student A can only answer *yes* or *no*.

● Check everyone knows the meaning of the words in the vocabulary box. Ask the students to guess which items you have in your bag or pocket. It may be amusing to produce some unlikely objects as well, such as, a candle, a pair of scissors, a clock.

● Ask the students if they have any of the items from the vocabulary box in their bags or pockets.

2 **Aim: to practise listening for main ideas; to review the vocabulary presented in the box.**
● 🔲 Ask the students to listen and put the number of the speaker by the item in the vocabulary box. Play the tape.

> **Answers**
> Speaker 1: keys
> Speaker 2: paperback novel
> Speaker 3: mobile phone
> Speaker 4: diary
> Speaker 5: chocolate
> Speaker 6: business card
> Speaker 7: a notebook, a ballpoint pen
> Speaker 8: penknife

3 **Aim: to check listening comprehension; to practise using the vocabulary presented in the box.**
● Ask the students to check their answers to activity 2 and to explain why the speakers never leave home without the item. Encourage them to remember as many details as possible.

4 **Aim: to provide an opportunity for a second listening.**

● 🔲 Play the tape again and ask them to check the details they mentioned in activity 3.

GRAMMAR

1 **Aim: to practise using *in case* or *if*.**
● Ask the students to read the information in the grammar box and then to do the exercises.

● Ask the students to write full answers to this exercise as it will be helpful for the *Sounds* activity.

> **Answers**
> 1 Can you collect me from the station **if** the train arrives late?
> 2 I'll take something to drink **in case** I get thirsty.
> 3 I'll arrive with plenty of local currency **in case** the airport bank is closed.
> 4 Can you get me some stamps **if** the post office is open.
> 5 He got to the station early **in case** he missed the train.
> 6 Use my pen **if** yours doesn't work.

2 **Aim: to practise using *in case*.**
● Ask the students to look back at their answers to *Vocabulary and listening* activity 3. Draw their attention to the example sentence with and then ask one or two students to do the first sentences orally.

● Ask the students to write full answers to *Vocabulary and listening* activity 3. You may like to suggest that they do this with another student.

3 Aim: to practise using *in case* and the vocabulary in the box.

● Ask the students to work alone and choose six items from the vocabulary box. Ask them to write sentences saying why it's a good idea to take them. You may also prefer to do this activity orally.

SOUNDS

Aim: to focus on stressed syllables in words.

● Ask the students to say which syllable is stressed in the words.
● 🔲 Play the tape and ask the students to check their answers. As they listen, ask them to say the words aloud.

READING

1 Aim: to prepare for reading; to pre-teach some unfamiliar words.

● Many of these words may be known to the students, but it's useful to check before they begin reading, since the meaning of the words allows access to the main ideas of the passage. If students are finding difficulty with unfamiliar vocabulary items, it will inhibit their comprehension of the reading passage.

2 Aim: to practise reading for main ideas.

● Ask the students to read the text and to match each paragraph with one of the items mentioned in activity 1.

3 Aim: to practise dealing with unfamiliar words.

● These words are not important for the student at this level, but the activity is designed to practise dealing with unfamiliar words so that they do not detract the reader from the general sense of the passage.

● Go through this activity with the whole class, but avoid giving an exact explanation of the meaning.

4 Aim: to practise using *in case*.

● Ask the students to read the passage again and to find the reasons why John Hatt takes the items.

SPEAKING

1 Aim: to practise speaking.

● Ask the students to list all the items they take on a car journey, a skiing trip or a walking holiday. Suggest other trips if these are not appropriate to your class.

● In pairs ask the students to explain to each other why they want to take these items.

2 Aim: to practise speaking.

● Ask the students to list all the things they never leave home without. Give them two minutes to do this.

● Tell the students to decide which items are essential. In pairs they compare their lists with their partner's.

● Ask the students to cover each other's lists and to write down their partner's list. How many items can they remember?

32
GENERAL COMMENTS

Complaining

This lesson focuses on ways of writing letters of complaint, which is a common task in language teaching contexts, but a rare one in real life. Making an effective complaint is difficult enough in one's own language, and infinitely more complex in a foreign language. So the lesson is designed more to expose the students to the type of language they would find in this situation and to discuss their attitudes towards complaining and complaints, rather than realistically expecting them to complain effectively themselves.

Letter writing

This lesson presents some of the common formulae used to open and close a letter. It is important to remind students that they should avoid translation of the equivalent formulae from their own language, as they will sound distorted and unnatural. It is also useful to point out that unless your students are preparing for a British or American exam, and as long as the information is clearly presented, there is no reason why the students should not use the conventions of letter layout (position of addresses, ways of writing the date etc) particular to their own language rather than adopt the British conventions. There are differences in American English: in dates, the month is put before the day; full points are used in all abbreviated titles, for example, *Mr., Mrs., Dr., Ms.;* a colon is used after a formal salutation, for example, *Dear Mr Smith:* and they finish with *Sincerely, Yours sincerely* but never *Yours faithfully.*

SPEAKING

1 Aim: to introduce the theme of the lesson; to practise speaking.
- Ask the students to think about their attitudes towards complaining. In which situations do they make a complaint? Ask them to think of specific occasions in the past when they made a complaint.

- Ask the students to tell the rest of the class about the last time they made a complaint.

2 Aim: to practise speaking
- Ask the students to discuss if they prefer to write letters of complaint or if they prefer to complain in person. Which do they think is more effective? Do they feel they need to be aggressive when they complain?

VOCABULARY

1 Aim: to present the vocabulary in the box; to pre-teach some unfamiliar words.
- The vocabulary field of cars and their equipment is a tightly defined and useful one. Ask the students which parts of the car they can see in the photo.

2 Aim: to practise writing definitions of unfamiliar vocabulary.
- Encourage the students to write definitions of six of the parts of the car they can't see, but without copying the definition from the dictionary. Suggest that they try to put the word into a meaningful example sentence.

READING AND LISTENING

1 Aim: to practise reading for main ideas.

● The sequence of the letters will be apparent once they have been carefully read. Ask the students to match the dates to the letters.

Answers
Letter c: 10 July
Letter a: 14 July
Letter e: 16 July
Letter b: 25 July
Letter d: 30 July

2 Aim: to practise listening for main ideas.

● ⬛ Ask the students to listen to the telephone dialogue and decide after which letter the conversation took place.

Answer
After Letter e sent on 16 July.

GRAMMAR

1 Aim: to practise using *due to* and *is/are likely to.*

● Ask the students to read the information in the grammar box, and then to do the exercises.

● Ask the students to write sentences about their own certain or probable futures.

● Ask the students to read out their sentences to the rest of the class.

2 Aim: to practise using *when, as soon as* and *after*.

● Ask the students to do this activity orally at first, and then ask them to write their answers.

Possible answers
1 **When** the spare parts arrive, we'll ring you.
2 **As soon as** we're less busy we'll contact you.
3 **After** you have received this letter, you can collect the car.
4 **When** you leave hospital, you can come to our showroom.
5 **As soon as** you come to our showroom, we'll show you a new car.
6 **After** I get better, I'll go and see my lawyer.

WRITING

1 Aim: to focus on letter writing conventions.

● Ask the students to think about the order in which they might see the features. Most of them are relevant to all formal letters. Suggest that they check their answers with the letters in this lesson and to see if there are any differences between their own letter-writing conventions and those in English.

Answers
your address
name and address of person you're sending it to
date
greetings
reason for writing
complaint
request for information or action
conclusion
closing remarks
your signature and name

2 Aim: to focus on letter writing complaints.

● Ask the students to look at the letters again and to find each of the features in activity 1.

● Ask them to find out how to start and finish a letter to someone whose name you know and you don't know.

Answer
Dear Sir or Madam
Dear (name)

3 Aim: to practise writing a letter of complaint.

● Ask the students to choose one of the situations and to write a suitable letter of complaint.

● You may like to ask the students to do this activity for homework.

33

GENERAL COMMENTS

Clauses of purpose

A typical mistake made by students is the use of *for* + infinitive or gerund, instead of *to* + infinitive.

For example, *For making your windows really shine, clean them with wet newspapers.* However, most students will have already come across all of these structures in isolation. This lesson is designed to focus on and compare their different uses.

VOCABULARY AND READING

1 Aim: to present the vocabulary in the box.

● The words in the box are those which are most often used in everyday household contexts. Students may be more familiar with some of them than others.

> **Answers**
> brush off, fly, limp, mark, mop up, polish, remove, scrape off, shine, sip, spread, stain, stretch, tie, wrap

● Check that everyone understands the other words.

2 Aim: to practise speaking; to prepare for reading.

● This activity is to encourage those students who have already acquired the target structures to use them before the consolidation work in the grammar section. But because they may not know the answers to the questions, it is also designed to set a task for reading. Ask them to read the questions and to guess the answers.

3 Aim: to practise reading for specific information.

● Ask the students to read the passage and to find the answers to the questions in activity 2.

● Don't check the answers yet because this will be done in *Grammar* activity 1.

● You may like to explain the following terms:

Dame: a title given to a woman who has been awarded a knighthood. Having received this title, she is allowed to sit in the House of Lords.
Marchioness: the wife of a Marquis, a hereditary title.
nanny: a woman who is paid to look after the young children of a family.
Right Honourable: a title for someone who is a politician and a member of the Privy Council, a special committee which advises the Queen.
Lord: a member of the House of Lords.
Field Marshall: the highest rank in the army.
HRH: His/Her Royal Highness, a title for members of the Queen's close family. HRH Princess Margaret is the Queen's sister.

4 Aim: to practise speaking; to check reading comprehension.

● Ask the students to decide which were the most useful and least useful hints. Which ones were more amusing or ridiculous? You may want to draw attention to the contrast between these extremely prosaic household hints and the high social status of the people who suggested them.

GRAMMAR

1 Aim: to practise using *to* + infinitive.

● Ask the students to read the information in the grammar box and then to do the exercises.

● Ask the students to think about their answers to *Vocabulary and reading* activity 2. Ask one or two students to give their answers and check they use *to* + infinitive correctly.

● Ask the students to write full answers to the questions. Make sure they place a comma between the two clauses.

> **Answers**
> 1 **To make** lettuce crisp again, place it in an empty saucepan with a lump of coal. After a few hours it will become crisp again.
> 2 **To avoid** rings after removing a stain, dry the spot quickly with a hairdryer.
> 3 **To make** your windows really shine, clean them with wet newspaper, then polish them with a soft cloth.
> 4 **To remove** red wine from a carpet, pour white wine on the stain and leave it for five or ten minutes before mopping it up.
> 5 **To clean** a burnt oven dish easily, put it face down on the grass all night.

2 Aim: to practise using *by* + *-ing*.

● Ask the students to rewrite their answers to activity 1 using *by* + *-ing*. You don't need to separate the clauses with a comma.

> **Answers**
> 1 **By placing** lettuce in an empty saucepan with a lump of coal you can make it crisp again.
> 2 **By drying** a damp spot quickly with a hairdryer you can avoid rings after removing a stain.
> 3 **By cleaning** your windows with wet newspaper and polishing them with a soft cloth you can make them really shine.
> 4 **By pouring** white wine on a red wine stain and leaving it for five minutes you can remove the stain very easily.
> 5 **By putting** a burnt dish face down on the grass all night you can easily clean it the next morning.

3 Aim: to practise giving advice with *if* + present simple.

● Ask the students to do this activity orally, then in writing.

> **Answers**
> 1 If your coffee loses its aroma, add a cube of plain chocolate just before using.
> 2 If you want to test if an egg is fresh, place it in a bowl of water. If the egg floats, it is bad.
> 3 If you want shiny, bright teeth, brush them occasionally with salt.
> 4 If you get food on your tie, soak it well with white wine.
> 5 If there are flies on your windscreen, put toothpaste on with a wet rag, wash it off and polish the glass with newspaper.

SOUNDS

1 Aim: to focus on different ways of pronouncing vowel sounds.

● The students will already have understood that the relationship between the spelling and the pronunciation of English words is not always obvious. Ask them to say the words aloud and choose one in which the vowel sound is different.

> **Answers**
> 1 water   2 ice   3 cube   4 spread

● 🔲 Play the tape and ask the students to listen and repeat the words.

2 Aim: to focus on weak forms.

● This activity focuses on the unstressed /ə/ and /ɪ/ sounds.

> **Answers**
> If lettuce becomes limp, place it in an empty saucepan with a lump of coal. Put the lid on, and after a few hours it will become crisp again. Fresh coffee, once opened, soon loses its aroma. By adding a cube of plain chocolate to coffee just before using, you can restore the aroma.

LISTENING AND WRITING

1 Aim: to practise the target structures; to prepare for listening.

● Ask the students to work in pairs and to give advice about the problems mentioned. Make sure they use one of the target structures.

2 Aim: to practise listening for specific information.

● 🔲 Ask the students to listen and check their answers to activity 1. Play the tape. The answers to the listening will be checked in the next activity.

3 Aim: to check listening comprehension; to practise writing.

● Ask the students to write out the advice they heard in activity 2.

> **Answers**
> If your new leather shoes feel a bit tight, pour a small amount of boiling water into each shoe in turn. Leave them for no more than six seconds, pour the water away and put on the shoes. The leather will have softened sufficiently for your feet to stretch them so that you no longer feel the pinch.
>
> To stop hiccups, block your nose and ears with your fingers and sip water at the same time. Someone else has to hold the glass, of course, so if it doesn't stop the hiccups at least everyone has a good laugh.
>
> If you have made a mark on a piece of wooden furniture (for example, a watermark), you can remove it by mixing some cigarette ash with some olive oil until it forms a paste. Spread this over the mark generously and leave it overnight to remove it. Next day the mark should have disappeared.
>
> To remove chewing gum from an item of clothing, place it in the freezer overnight. The following day, the chewing gum can be easily scraped off. The same principle applies to gum on carpet. Rub it with an ice cube until the gum is solid and then scrape it off.

4 Aim: to practise speaking; to practise using the target structures.

● Ask the students to work in pairs. They should choose two or three of the situations and then should note down some advice.

5 Aim: to practise speaking; to practise using the target structures.

● Ask the students to go round giving and collecting Superhints from the others. Which students have suggested the most useful Superhints?

6 Aim: to practise writing; to practise using the target structures.

● Ask the students to work in groups and compile a list of Superhints for the class.

● You may like to ask the students to do this activity for homework.

34

GENERAL COMMENTS

The conditional

This will not be the first time the students have come across conditional sentences. In Lesson 31, the zero conditional was presented. In *Reward* Pre-intermediate, the first and second conditionals were presented as well, so this lesson may be revision for some students. In his excellent book *Grammar Games* (Cambridge University Press), Mario Rinvolucri rightly, although somewhat forcefully, writes that the terms first, second and third conditional 'are misleading terms, resulting from pedagogically motivated simplification of descriptive grammar. In real life English, native speakers use all kinds of conditional combinations which go way beyond the neat, mendacious packaging of the three conditional patterns.' He then gives a series of examples in which an *if* clause + past simple is followed by a present simple, and *if* + *going to* is followed by a simple past, a mixture of third and second conditional, a mixture of second and first conditional. In *Reward*, the terms are nevertheless used for 'pedagogically motivated' reasons in a more positive sense of the term: they are how most teachers refer to the structures, they are what the teachers expect students to learn, and they are the three main patterns which are the most common, and which students confuse most often.

READING AND VOCABULARY

1 Aim: to introduce the theme of the lesson.

● Before the students open their books, write on the board the word *green*. Ask the students to think of words they associate with *green*, and write them on the board.

● Explain that the theme of the lesson is environmentally friendly tourism, or 'green tourism'. Ask the students to make a list of the advantages and disadvantages of tourism in general. What do they think is meant by *green tourism?*

2 Aim: to practise reading for main ideas.

● Ask the students if they know about eco-tourism, which is being environmentally friendly to the place you visit as a tourist. It isn't just a matter of taking home your rubbish, it's also about supporting the local economy and not demanding the equipment and installations which you would expect at home but which would be out of place in the tourist destination.

● Ask the students to read the passage and decide if they are good or bad tourists.

● When they have read the text, ask them to discuss whether they follow the advice given in the passage. Do the students agree with the advice in the passage?

3 Aim: to practise reading for specific information.

● Explain that the text talks about the economic, cultural or environmental effects of tourism. Ask the students to read the text again and to decide if each piece of advice is economic, cultural or environmental.

Answers
1 environmental 2 economic 3 economic
4 cultural 5 cultural 6 cultural 7 cultural
8 environmental 9 economic 10 cultural

4 Aim: to give an opportunity for a second reading.

● Ask the students to look at the passage and decide where the sentences can go.

Answers
a 10 b 6 c 8 d 4

5 Aim: to present the vocabulary in the box; to exploit unfamiliar words from the passage; to focus on collocation.

● Ask the students to check they understand all the new words which come from the passage.

● In pairs encourage them to explore possible collocations. Check this activity with the whole class.

GRAMMAR

1 Aim: to focus on the first conditional.

● Ask the students to read the information in the grammar box and then to do the exercises.

● Make it quite clear that the tense in the *if* clause is the present simple, and in the main clause the future simple.

● This activity will be used in *Sounds* activity 2, so it may be a good idea to ask students to write it out in full.

Possible answers
1 f 2 e 3 d 4 c 5 b 6 a

Some variations are possible. Discuss these as you correct the exercise.

2 Aim: to practise using the first conditional.

● Ask the students to complete the sentences with their own plans.

3 Aim: to practise using the first conditional.

● Ask the students to rewrite the advice given in the passage using a first conditional. Some variation is possible.

1 If you use public transport, there will be less
   pollution.
2 If you stay in small hotels and eat local food, your
   money will stay in the local area.
3 If you travel out of season, it will be cheaper and
   you'll avoid the crowds.
4 If you think of yourself as a guest, you'll have a
   different relationship with your hosts.
5 If you don't learn the language, you won't be able
   to talk to the local people.
6 If you aren't careful about taking photos in some
   places, people will be embarrassed or will ask you
   for money.
7 If you find out about the place you're visiting, the
   local people will appreciate your good manners.
8 If you use less water, there will be enough for
   local people.
9 If you use local guides, it will create jobs and help
   the local economy.
10 If you adopt the local lifestyle, you'll enjoy
   yourself much more.

SOUNDS

1 Aim: to focus on the /ɪ/ sound.
● 📼 Play the tape and ask the students to repeat
the phrases.

**2 Aim: to focus on intonation in conditional
sentences.**
● Write one or two of the sentences from *Grammar*
activity 1 on the board, and ask one or two students to
say them aloud. Try and help them predict the
intonation pattern. Ask them to predict which words are
likely to be stressed.

● 📼 Ask the students to follow the sentences they
wrote in *Grammar* activity 1 as they listen to the tape.
Play the tape.

● 📼 Ask the students to say the sentences aloud. Play
the tape a second time.

LISTENING AND SPEAKING

1 Aim: to practise speaking.
● Ask the students to look at the photos in this lesson.
Ask the students if they would like to visit any of these
places. What kind of holiday do they like? Why?

2 Aim: to practise speaking.
● Ask the students to look at the list and decide which
they like doing when they go on holiday. Find out
what the majority of the class think about each aspect
of tourism.

**3 Aim: to prepare for listening; to present the
language to illustrate the target structures.**
● Explain that you are going to play a recording in
which two people talk about their plans to visit Nepal.
Ask the students to read the statements and match the
situations with the possible results.

Answers
1 g   2 d   3 b   4 h   5 a   6 e   7 f   8 i   9 j   10 c

● There may be more than one possibility, which will
encourage more careful listening.

● 📼 Ask the students to listen and check their
answers. Play the tape.

● Don't correct this activity yet as students will use it
for discussion in the next activity.

**4 Aim: to practise speaking; to practise using
the first conditional.**
● Ask the students to work in pairs, and to use the
situations and results to give advice to Max and Susie.
Make sure they use first conditionals.

Answers
1 If they visit Nepal in April, they'll have
   bad weather.
2 If they go there in August, they'll have
   good weather.
3 If they travel out of season, they'll avoid the
   crowds, and it'll be cheaper.
4 If they fly there, they'll get there quicker.
5 If they drive overland, they'll travel around
   more easily.
6 If they stay in hotels, they'll spend a lot of money.
7 If they go camping, they'll save money.
8 If they take their own food, they'll have a
   lot to carry.
9 If they pay for their holiday in Britain, they'll
   use British money.
10 If they take a guide book, they'll avoid hiring
   a local guide.

● Check that everyone pauses (the spoken equivalent
of a comma between the two clauses).

5 Aim: to practise speaking.
● Lead a class discussion on what should be done to
help relieve the effects of tourism on towns in the
students' countries. What are the main tourist
destinations? What can be done to make life easier in
those places? Should tourists be encouraged or
discouraged from visiting them?

● You may like to ask students to write a paragraph
about the results of the discussion for homework.

35

GENERAL COMMENTS

Past perfect

Students often use the present perfect when a past perfect is more suitable, especially in reported speech, for example, *He said he has already left*. Similarly, a past perfect is sometimes used where a present perfect should appear, for example, *I had given it to you already. What had you done with it?* Students who have followed *Reward* Pre-intermediate will have already seen the past perfect in isolation, and it appeared in Lessons 23, 24 and 25 of this book in reported speech. This lesson revises the use of the tense to describe actions which happened before other actions in the past.

READING

1 Aim: to read for main ideas.

● The passage is quite long and it's important that the students get the main ideas before they try to understand it in greater detail. Try not to answer vocabulary questions until they have done this activity.

> **Answer**
> The original title was *The unsolved mystery*.

2 Aim: to provide an opportunity for a second reading; to establish the sequence of events; to prepare for *Grammar* activity 1.

● In order to be able to use the past perfect successfully, it's important that the students are clear about the sequence of events.

> **Answers**
> 1 learned to fly
> 2 established a new altitude record
> 3 became first woman to fly the Atlantic
> 4 set a women's speed record
> 5 married George Putnam
> 6 flew coast-to-coast across the USA
> 7 achieved a Pacific speed record
> 8 disappeared in the Pacific

GRAMMAR

1 Aim: to practise using *after* + past perfect.

● Ask the students to read the information in the grammar box and then to do the exercises.

● Ask the students to do this activity orally at first.

> **Answers**
> 1 After she **had learnt** to fly, she **established** a new altitude record.
> 2 After she **had become** the first woman to fly the Atlantic, she **set** a women's speed record.
> 3 After she **had married** George Putnam, she **flew** coast-to-coast across the USA.
> 4 After she **had achieved** a Pacific speed record, she **disappeared** in the Pacific.

2 Aim: to focus on the sequence of tenses.

● Ask the students to explain what the difference between the two sentences is.

> **Answers**
> **Sentence a** means she disappeared, then, afterwards, she grew tired of her fame.
>
> **Sentence b** is true. First, she grew tired of her fame, then she disappeared.

3 Aim: to focus on the past perfect simple and continuous.

● Remind the students that they may wish to focus on the continuation of an action in the past rather than a completed event. The distinction is similar to the use of all continuous formed sentences. Remind students we are still talking about a 'before past' event.

> **Answers**
> 1 Amelia **had been living** in Kansas for 23 years when she **went** to California.
> 2 Because she **had spent** an unhappy childhood, she **didn't visit** her family.
> 3 She **had grown** tired of being famous when she decided to retire.
> 4 She **had been flying** for seventeen years when she **disappeared.**

4 Aim: to practise using *because* + past perfect.

● Ask the students to think about their answers to the questions and to speculate about Amelia Earhart's fate.

● If there is time, ask the students to write full answers to the questions.

> **Possible answers**
> 1 Because she had had an unhappy childhood.
> 2 Because she had grown tired of her fame.
> 3 Because the US Navy had been receiving SOS messages for several days.
>
> The students can speculate as to the answer to 4.

VOCABULARY AND WRITING

1 Aim: to present the vocabulary in the box; to focus on the new vocabulary from the passage.

● Ask the students to check they understand the new words from the story. Ask them to think of the sentence they found them in. Turn this into a competition. Put students into pairs. Ask them to remember the sentence in the passage where the word was used. Score a point for each correct sentence. The students who have most points are the winners.

● Encourage the students to add words to their *Wordbanks*.

2 Aim: to practise writing.

● Ask the students to work in groups of three or four and to talk about other unsolved mysteries. They should collect together as many details as possible and then write a paragraph describing the unsolved mystery.

Progress check Lessons 31–35

GENERAL COMMENTS

You can work through this Progress check in the order shown, or concentrate on areas which may have caused difficulty in Lessons 31 to 35. You can also let the students choose the activities they would like to or feel the need to do.

VOCABULARY

1 Aim: to focus on words borrowed from other languages.

● Your students may have noticed that their own languages have borrowed many English words. Ask them to suggest a few.

● It is also important to point out that English has borrowed many words from other languages. Ask them to guess which languages the loan words come from.

Answers
chilli (Spanish), pasta (Italian),
casserole (French), cuisine (French),
hamburger (German), avocado (Spanish),
tacos (Spanish), goulash (Hungarian),
kebab (Turkish), delicatessen (German),
samovar (Russian), omelette (French),
spaghetti (Italian), frankfurter (German)

● Ask the students to think about other types of loan words in their own language.

2 Aim: to focus on words which go in pairs.

● Ask the students to use their dictionary to find out the natural order of the words.

Answers
1 bread and butter
2 fish and chips
3 toast and jam
4 bacon and eggs
5 milk and sugar
6 tea and biscuits
7 apples and pears
8 strawberries and cream
9 bread and cheese
10 salt and pepper
11 oil and vinegar
12 fruit and vegetables

3 Aim: to focus on antonyms.

● The students have already come across opposites, but the suggestion here is that they should note down any possible antonyms as they come across them.

Answers
arrival – departure, round trip – single,
exciting – boring, child – adult,
lucky – unlucky, number – letter, freezing – boiling,
sweet – sour, finger – thumb,
buy – sell, officer – soldier, fictional – factual,
dirty – clean, funny – serious, disappear – appear,
customer – salesperson, laugh – cry,
poverty – wealth, ceiling – floor

4 Aim: to record words in the students' *Wordbanks*.

● Give the students five or ten minutes to look back at the vocabulary boxes in Lessons 31 to 35 and to write them in suitable categories in their *Wordbanks*.

GRAMMAR

1 Aim: to revise the difference between *in case* and *if*.

Answers
1 I'll take some food **in case** I get hungry.
2 Can you buy me a loaf **if** the shop is open?
3 There may be a pool at the hotel, so pack your swimming costume **in case** there is.
4 She always walked slowly **if** there was snow on the ground.
5 I'll pack my favourite soap **in case** I can't get any while I'm there.
6 I'll buy a new car **if** I have enough money.

2 Aim: to revise *when, after* and *as soon as*.

● Ask the students to write their own answers to these questions.

3 Aim: to revise the first conditional.

Answers
1 If you leave now, you'll catch the train.
2 If you stay in bed, you'll feel better.
3 If you work hard, you'll get a better job.
4 If you eat carrots, you'll be able to see in the dark.
5 If you go shopping, you'll spend a lot of money.
6 If you ride a bike, you'll save energy.

4 Aim: to revise *by* + *-ing*.

Answers

1 By leaving now, you'll catch the train.
2 By staying in bed, you'll feel better.
3 By working hard, you'll get a better job.
4 By eating carrots, you'll be able to see in the dark.
5 By going shopping, you'll spend a lot of money.
6 By riding a bike, you'll save energy.

5 Aim: to revise *because* and *when* with the past perfect.

Answers

1 Because they had left the window open, someone broke into their house.
2 Because she had had a busy day, she went to bed early.
3 When he arrived at the station, the train had already left.
4 Because we had had a good meal, I left a large tip.
5 Because she had lost her chequebook, she couldn't write a cheque.
6 Because the phone had rung several times without any answer, he hung up.

SOUNDS

1 Aim: to focus on the different ways of pronouncing the letter *o*.

● Ask the students to say the words aloud and then group the words according to the pronunciation of the letter *o*.

Answers

/ɒ/: popular spot clock
/əʊ/: photo solo mobile phone
/ʌ/: one done
/uː/: lose
/ɔː/: afford torn

● 📼 Play the tape and ask the students to repeat the words.

2 Aim: to focus on the shift of stress in nouns and verbs.

● 📼 Play the tape and ask the students to underline the stressed syllable.

Answers

to sus<u>pect</u> – a <u>sus</u>pect   to pro<u>test</u> – a <u>pro</u>test
to re<u>ject</u> – a <u>re</u>ject   to in<u>crease</u> – an <u>in</u>crease
to ex<u>port</u> – an <u>ex</u>port   to re<u>cord</u> – a <u>re</u>cord
to pre<u>sent</u> – a <u>pre</u>sent   to pro<u>duce</u> – <u>pro</u>duce

● In two-syllable words, which can be both verb and noun, the stress goes on the first syllable in the nouns, and the second syllable in the verbs.

3 Aim: to focus on syllable stress.

● Ask the students to listen and repeat the words focusing on the stressed syllable.

Answers

con<u>sump</u>tion eco<u>no</u>mic em<u>bar</u>rass hos<u>pit</u>able
<u>head</u>light spee<u>do</u>meter <u>wind</u>screen <u>in</u>dicator
<u>thunder</u>storn <u>dan</u>ger disa<u>ppear</u> in<u>diff</u>erent
e<u>qua</u>tor fru<u>stra</u>tion propa<u>gan</u>da pro<u>tec</u>tion

SPEAKING AND LISTENING

1 Aim: to practise speaking.

● Explain that there is some advice which is wrong, and some advice which may be surprising but true.
Ask the students to read the advice and to guess which is the false advice.

2 Aim: to practise speaking; to practise using zero and first conditional sentences.

● It's more likely that the first conditional would be more common in discussing an unlikely situation and its consequences, but on occasions a zero conditional is acceptable. Ask the students to discuss the advice and its possible consequences.

3 Aim: to practise listening for main ideas.

● 📼 During this first listening activity, the aim is simply to find out if the advice is true or false. Play the tape and ask the students to check their answers to activity 1.

4 Aim: to practise speaking; to practise listening for specific information.

● Ask the students to try to remember what John said about the possible consequences of following or not following each piece of advice.

● 📼 Play the tape again and ask the students to check their answers.

36
GENERAL COMMENTS

Relationships

Another popular topic among students, especially teenagers, is relationships. The topic has been chosen to make use of this important source of motivation. You may need to explain the convention of the *Problem page,* which provides the reading material in this lesson. A *Problem page* is something which can be found in magazines, and gives readers the opportunity to write to the *Agony aunt* or *uncle* for advice about a particular problem, often something to do with relationships.

Second conditional

Most students will have come across the second conditional by now, and this lesson is designed to revise and extend their knowledge of how it's used. Remind students that the *if* clause can come at the beginning or the end of the sentence, and that *If I were you,* is a common set phrase (*were* is the subjunctive form of *was)*. The verb in the *if* clause is often in the past simple, but can also be in other past tenses.

READING AND VOCABULARY

1 **Aim: to present the vocabulary in the box; to pre-teach some important words.**

● Ask the class if they know what an *Agony aunt* is. Who is she? Who writes to her? Ask them if they know what a *Problem page* is? Where would you find a *Problem page?*

● Ask the students to look at the words in the box and to focus on the verb and verb phrases. These can all refer to different stages of a relationship. Ask the students to put them in the right order.

● Ask the students to put the nouns with the verbs. There may be more than one possible answer.

> **Possible answers**
> **verb and verb phrases:**
> meet someone, get to know someone,
> fancy someone, ask someone out,
> go out with, get involved with someone,
> fall in love with, get engaged,
> get married, lie about something,
> do something behind someone's back,
> fall out with someone, feel jealous, break up
>
> **stages of a relationship and possible nouns:**
> meet someone – acquaintance
> get to know someone – friend
> get involved with someone – girlfriend, boyfriend
> get engaged to someone – fiancé(e)
> get married – partner

2 **Aim: to practise reading for main ideas.**

● Explain that the letters and the replies are mixed up. Ask the students to read the letters and to match them with the correct replies.

> **Answers**
> 1 e 2 a 3 b 4 c 5 d

3 Aim: to practise speaking; to read for specific information; to read and infer.

● Explain that it would be very unlikely that a series of people would all write to the problem page of a magazine about the same interlinked problem, but that this fiction is designed to not simply be amusing but to motivate the students to read and infer who is who.

> **Answer**
> **Letter 1:** Julia is going out with Barry.
> **Letter 2:** Barry's ex-girlfriend is Sharon.
> **Letter 3:** Tony's best friend is Barry, and Julia keeps flirting with him.
> **Letter 4 :** Sharon's ex-boyfriend is Barry.
> **Letter 5:** Steve is falling in love with Julia.

GRAMMAR

1 Aim: to present the second conditional.

● Ask the students to read the explanation in the grammar box and then do the exercises.

● Ask the students to think of suitable reactions to the situations described and to write sentences using second conditionals.

2 Aim: to practise giving advice.

● Make sure the students use the three expressions in turn when they give advice.

SOUNDS

Aim: to focus on linked sounds in connected speech.

● Remind students that words are linked in connected speech in English. Ask them to predict which words the speaker will link. You may want to remind them of the rules for linking in Progress checks 6–10 and 11–15.

> **Answers**
>
> 1 If I were you, I'd invite him in.
>
> 2 In my opinion, you ought to eat it all up.
>
> 3 If I were you, I wouldn't even answer.
>
> 4 In my opinion, you ought to wear a suit.
>
> 5 If I were you, I'd turn on the heating.

● Play the tape and ask the students to listen and check their answers. Ask them to say the sentences aloud.

LISTENING AND WRITING

1 Aim: to prepare for listening.

● Ask the students to read the situations and to decide what they would do. You may like to ask the class for their advice.

2 Aim: to listen for main ideas.

● Play the tape and ask the students to decide which situation the speakers are discussing.

> **Answer**
> Situation 2

3 Aim: to practise writing.

● Ask the students to choose one of the situations discussed in activity 1 and write a letter giving their advice.

● You may like to ask the students to do this activity for homework.

37

GENERAL COMMENTS

Hong Kong

You may want to give your students some extra information about Hong Kong. Hong Kong Island is one of the most densely inhabited places in the world and is an important business centre. On the mainland opposite is Kowloon, with its shopping and tourist centres, and beyond that, high-rise commercial and industrial estates. Beyond Kowloon lie the New Territories. In all, Hong Kong covers 1070 sq kilometres. The official population is about 5.8 million.

VOCABULARY AND READING

1 Aim: to present the words in the vocabulary box; to pre-teach some important words; to prepare for reading.

● Ask the students if they know where Hong Kong is. How many people live there? What's special about Hong Kong? Would they like to go there?

● Ask the students to put the words in the box under the headings where appropriate. They may like to do this in pairs.

> **Possible answers**
> **Where to stay:** accommodation, lobby
> **What to do:** view, relax
> **What to buy:** silk, porcelain
> **When to go:** peak season, summer, autumn
> **What to eat:** dish
> **What to wear:** bikini, miniskirt, shorts, sandals
> **Where to go:** junk, harbour, shopping mall

2 Aim: to read for main ideas.

● This matching activity, like most matching activities, is designed to discourage the students from trying to understand every word. Make sure they complete this activity before you answer any vocabulary questions. If possible, wait until after activity 3.

> **Answers**
> **Paragraph 1:** when to go
> **Paragraph 2:** where to go
> **Paragraph 3:** where to stay
> **Paragraph 4:** what to wear
> **Paragraph 5:** what to eat
> **Paragraph 6:** what to buy
> **Paragraph 7:** what to do
>
> Some of the vocabulary in activity 1 may have gone under different headings.

3 Aim: to focus on techniques for dealing with unfamiliar words.

● These questions are designed to help the students work out the general meaning of some new words. There's no need to insist that they find an exact translation for these words, and it's probably better if they don't write them down.

4 Aim: to read for specific information; to provide an opportunity for a second reading.

● This activity will allow the students to take a more detailed look at the passage.

● You may want to check the answers with the whole class.

> **Answers**
> 1 True
> 2 True
> 3 False
> 4 True – with the exception of flip-flop sandals
> 5 The passage infers this is true
> 6 True
> 7 True

LISTENING

1 Aim: to listen for specific information.

● ▭ Ask the students to listen and find out which things mentioned in the reading passage Jill did while she was in Hong Kong.

> **Answers**
> She went in the summer, went sightseeing, went up the Peak, visited Aberdeen, ate *dim sum,* went shopping, spent too much money.

2 Aim: to check comprehension; to provide an opportunity for a second listening.

● Ask the students to work in pairs and check their answers to 1. Which of the things in the Factfile didn't she do?

> **Answers**
> She didn't stay in a hotel, or on Hong Kong Island. She didn't go in the autumn, or go to the beach, or take a trip to the New Territories.

● ▭ Play the tape again and ask the students to check their answers.

GRAMMAR

1 Aim: to practise using *should* or *shouldn't have*.

● Ask the students to read the explanation in the grammar box and then do the exercises.

● Ask the students to write sentences using suitable past modal verbs.

> **Answers**
> 1 I shouldn't have walked. I should have taken the car.
> 2 You shouldn't have waited.
> 3 He shouldn't have eaten so much.
> 4 They shouldn't have spent so long in the sun.
> 5 You should have been here last week.
> 6 I shouldn't have bought so much.

2 Aim: to practise using *should* or *shouldn't have*.

● Ask the students to work in pairs, and to look back at their answers to *Listening* activities 1 and 2.

> **Answers**
> She shouldn't have gone in the summer. She should have gone when it was cooler.
> She should have spent some time on Hong Kong Island or in Kowloon.
> She should have visited the New Territories.
> She should have taken a ferry to the islands.
> She shouldn't have worn flip-flops in the the restaurant.
> She shouldn't have eaten so much.
> She shouldn't have spent so much money.

SPEAKING

1 Aim: to practise speaking; to practise using *should* and *shouldn't have*.

● Ask the students to think about situations when they did something wrong. They should use the prompts to help them. At this stage they should work alone and think of as many situations as possible.

2 Aim: to practise speaking; to practise using *should* and *shouldn't have*.

● Ask the students to talk about the situations they thought of in activity 1.

● You may like to ask the students to write about their situations for homework.

38

GENERAL COMMENTS

Past modals

The students will already have practised using past modal verbs in Lesson 37. Remind them that modal verbs have no infinitives, that questions and negatives are formed without *do,* and that they are followed by the infinitive without *to* (except *ought).* Modals are usually used to refer to the present or the future. Modals + perfect infinitives are used for speculating or imagining situations in the past.

READING AND SPEAKING

1 Aim: to prepare for reading; to practise speaking.

● Ask the students to speculate about the answers to these questions about a passage. The passage itself appears in activity 2, but is scrambled. If you like, you can ask them to write full answers to the questions but leaving blanks if they cannot guess anything. When they read the passage, all they will need to do is use the information in the passage to fill in the blanks.

2 Aim: to read for text organisation.

● The sentences in this passage have been printed in the wrong order. Ask the students to read them and to put them in the right order.

> **Answers**
> d a c b

GRAMMAR

1 Aim: to focus on the uses of *may have, must have, might have, can't have*.

● Ask the students to read the explanation in the grammar box and then do the exercises.

● These structures can be confusing as some mean the same and others mean the exact opposite. Do this activity orally, and ask the students to explain what the sentences mean.

> **Answers**
> *It could have been* and *might have been a ghost* mean the same, that is, it was possibly a ghost, but we aren't sure.
> *It must have been a ghost* means it almost certainly was a ghost.
> *It can't have been a ghost* means it almost certainly wasn't a ghost.

2 Aim: to practise using *might have* and *could have*.

● If your students are manipulating the structure successfully, do this exercise orally.

> **Possible answers**
> 1 I might have left it at home.
> 2 It could have run out of petrol.
> 3 She might have missed the train.
> 4 He could have gone out.
> 5 She could have fallen asleep.
> 6 He could have gone for a bike ride.

3 Aim: to practise using *must have* and *can't have*.

● Do this activity orally with the whole class.

> **Possible answers**
> 1 She must have been ill.
> 2 He can't have got enough sleep.
> 3 She must have had some bad news.
> 4 They must have missed it.
> 5 He can't have knocked it over on purpose.
> 6 It must have been raining.

4 Aim: to practise speaking; to practise using the target structures.

● Ask the students to discuss what might/could/must or can't have happened in *Reading and speaking* activity 2.

● Ask the students to turn to Communication activity 16 on page 102 to find out what happened.

READING

Aim: to read for text organisation.

● This is a jigsaw-reading activity. Put the students into pairs, Student A and Student B. Explain to the students that they are going to read more stories about people who disappeared, but they will read different stories. Tell Student A to turn to Communication activity 4 on page 99 and Student B should turn to Communication activity 12 on page 101 and follow the instructions. These are both gap fill exercises.

> **Answers**
> **Student A:** 1 b 2 a 3 e 4 c 5 g 6 f 7 d
> **Student B:** 1 b 2 f 3 g 4 d 5 a 6 e 7 c

SPEAKING AND VOCABULARY

1 Aim: to practise speaking.

● Ask the students to tell their partners about the stories they have just read in *Reading*.

2 Aim: to practise speaking; to practise using the target structures.

● Ask the students in their pairs to speculate about the stories they have read or heard.

3 Aim: to practise speaking; to read for specific information.

● Ask the students to turn to Communication activity 17 on page 102 and find out the explanations for the stories.

4 Aim: to present the words in the vocabulary box.

● The students have already come across these words in the stories. They are presented in the box so that they can be noted down properly. The activity gives them an opportunity to use the target structures.

> **Answers**
> **First story:** clue, disappear, face, floor, lock, moan, mysteriously, seal, tiles, youngster
> **Student A's story:** disappear, disaster, plague
> **Student B's story:** assume, bandage, chatter, companion, cover, explore, manhole, pay attention, side street

5 Aim: to practise speaking.

● Ask the students to talk about other strange stories which they may know about. Tell them to look at the list of suggestions if they can't think of anything.

● Ask the students in each group to choose the strangest story and then tell the rest of the class about it.

● You may like to ask the students to choose one of the stories they have discussed and to write it up for homework.

39
GENERAL COMMENTS

Cross-cultural training

The focus of this lesson is to provide information about the British and North American educational systems and to allow students to reflect on their own culture, both in its educational system and in its attitudes towards education. So the subject matter is not presented merely to provide information about two foreign cultures. It serves as a mirror for the students' own cultures.

Wish

Students may have come across the rather formal use of *wish* meaning *want*, for example, *I wish to leave the room*. When used in this way, it is always followed by to + infinitive. When we use *wish* meaning *want things to be different from how they are* the verb which follows *wish* does not have the tense which corresponds to the meaning, but one which is 'more past'.

VOCABULARY AND LISTENING

1 **Aim: to present the words in the vocabulary box; to prepare for listening.**
  ● Explain that although the two education systems in Britain and North America are slightly different, there are some terms which are specific to both countries. Ask the students if they recognise which words are North American and which are English. Some words belong to both boxes, but may have a different meaning.

> **Answers**
> **British:** kindergarten, grade, primary school, middle school, secondary school, comprehensive school, public school, boarding school
> **American:** kindergarten, grade, grade school, elementary school, junior high school, high school, public school

2 **Aim: to listen for specific information.**
  ● 🔲 The two speakers are going to describe what the vocabulary in the box means. Play the tape once and ask the students to listen and mark them US or GB.

> **Answers**
> See activity 1.

  ● Ask the students to try to remember the meaning of the words. You may like to play the tape a second time.

3 **Aim: to present the vocabulary in the box; to prepare for listening; to pre-teach some important words.**
  ● These words may go under different headings according to the educational system. Ask the students to put them under the headings which correspond to their own country. The answer below is for Britain.

> **Possible answers for Britain**
> **Primary:** art, geography, history, music, physical education, science and technology, maths, physics, computer studies, reading, writing
> **Secondary:** art, geography, history, music, physical education, science and technology, maths, languages, chemistry, physics, car repairs, economics, computer studies, typing
> **University/college:** art, geography, history, music, physical education, science and technology, maths, languages, chemistry, physics, economics, computer studies, law, medicine, philosophy

  ● Ask the students to talk about other possible subjects to study at school or university. Suggest some practical disciplines like *home economics*.

4 **Aim: to practise listening for specific information.**
  ● 🔲 Explain that you're going to play a tape in which the two people in the photo talk about the educational systems in Britain and North America. Ask the students to work in pairs and to turn to the relevant Communication activity. Make sure they understand that they should only listen for the information they are directed to by the instructions. Play the tape.

5 **Aim: to check comprehension.**
  ● Ask the students to work together. The information they obtained separately should allow them to complete the chart together.

> **Answers**
> **Britain**
> Starting age: 5
> Leaving age: 16
> Examinations, type and age: 7,10,14,16
> Corporal punishment: None
> Homework: Half an hour a day
> Classroom participation: A little
> Payment of university fees: Local education authority
> Entrance requirements: An offer based on condition you obtain certain grades in 'A' Levels
>
> **USA**
> Starting age: 5
> Leaving age: 16
> Examinations, type and age: Throughout an educational career
> Corporal punishment: None
> Homework: An hour a day
> Classroom participation: A lot
> Payment of university fees: Parents
> Entrance requirements: High school grade point average, achievement tests, the SAT test scores

GRAMMAR

1 Aim: to focus on the uses of *wish*.

● Ask the students to read the explanation in the grammar box and then do the exercises.

● Ask the students to decide which sentences express a wish for the present or future and a regret about the past.

> **Answers**
> **Sentence a** is a wish for the present and future, *If I spoke English, I would be able to travel/speak to people.*
> **Sentence b** is a regret about the past, *If had spoken English, I would have been able to travel/speak to people.*

2 Aim: to focus on wishes for the present and future and regrets about the past.

● Ask the students to write sentences explaining the meaning of the sentences.

> **Answers**
> 1 I'd like to be able to type.
> 2 I didn't learn to play the piano and I regret it.
> 3 I'd like to live in America, but I don't.
> 4 I smoke, and I'd like to stop.
> 5 I didn't stay in touch and I regret it.
> 6 I'd like to travel round the world.

3 Aim: to focus on wishes for the present and future and regrets about the past.

● Do this activity in writing, as it will be useful for students to see the sentences in *Sounds* activity 2. You may like to point out that *if only* is stronger than *I wish*, and suggests a yearning rather than a desire or regret.

> **Answers**
> **Wishes for present and future:** 1, 3, 4, 6
> **Regrets about the past:** 2, 5
>
> 1 If only I could type.
> 2 If only I had learnt to play the piano.
> 3 If only I lived in America.
> 4 If only I didn't smoke.
> 5 If only I had stayed in touch with my school friends.
> 6 If only I could travel round the world.

4 Aim: to practise using *wish*.

● Ask the students to think about Frances and John's regrets about their education. Make sure they use sentences with *wish*.

> **Answers**
> **Frances wishes:** there had been some practical skills such as typing or cooking.
> She had taken time off between school and university.
> She hadn't gone to university at such a young age.

> **John wishes:** university hadn't been so expensive for his parents.
> He had got a scholarship.
> He had worked harder.

● 🔲 Play the tape again for the students to check their answers.

SOUNDS

1 Aim: to focus on changes in the pronunciation of '*d* in connected speech.

● 🔲 Remind the students that the '*d* sound often disappears in connected speech. Ask them to tick the sentences they hear.

● Ask the students to repeat the sentences.

> **Answers**
> I wish I'd worked harder.
> If only I walked to work.
> I wish I kept my temper.
> If only she'd paid me.
> I wish I had a dog.
> If only he'd like me.

2 Aim: to focus on strong stress and intonation in *if only* sentences.

● 🔲 Ask the students to listen to how the speaker uses strong stress and intonation for deep regrets and strong wishes. Play the tape and ask them to say the sentences aloud.

> **Answers**
> If only I could type.
> If only I had learnt to play the piano.
> If only I lived in America.
> If only I didn't smoke.
> If only I had stayed in touch with my school friends.
> If only I could travel round the world.

WRITING AND SPEAKING

1 Aim: to prepare for speaking and writing.

● Ask the students to list what they consider to be their educational achievements. Ask them to think about anything they regret or things they would like to have done differently.

2 Aim: to practise speaking.

● Ask the students to discuss their educational regrets using *wish*.

3 Aim: to practise writing; to practise using link words *like* and *but unlike*.

● The vocabulary and the information in the chart will give the students a good framework for this writing activity. Encourage them to make a comparison between the two systems (either Britain OR North America and their own) and to focus on similarities and differences.

● This activity can be done for homework.

40

GENERAL COMMENTS

The man who was everywhere

The story is by Edward D Hoch and was first published in 1957. It was taken from a collection of stories called *Stories my mother never told me,* which was edited by the director of thriller films, Alfred Hitchcock. It is easy to picture the story filmed by Hitchcock, and has a typical series of thrills, climaxes, twists to the story and an unexpected ending.

Third conditional

This is the last major structure in *Reward* Intermediate. The third conditional is sometimes called the *unreal past* conditional. Note that you can use the modal verbs *might* and *could* instead of *would* in the main clause. As with other conditionals, other tenses, such as progressives, are possible in both clauses, but the combinations presented in this lesson are the ones which cause students most problems. Exceptionally, the structure is presented at the beginning of the lesson because it would detract from the enjoyment of the story if presented in its usual position, that is to say, in the middle of the lesson.

GRAMMAR

1 Aim: to practise using the third conditional.

● Ask the students to read the explanation in the grammar box and to do the exercises.

● You may like to do this activity orally.

> **Answers**
> 1 If Giles had caught the plane, he wouldn't have spent his holiday at home.
> 2 If Brenda hadn't forgotten her chequebook, she would have bought us lunch.
> 3 If Jane had stayed at home, she wouldn't have felt so ill.
> 4 If Andrea had listened to the radio, she would have heard the bad news.
> 5 If the police had arrived quickly, they would have caught the burglar.
> 6 If Karim had spoken English, he would have made himself understood.

2 Aim: to practise using the third conditional.

● Ask the students to think about memorable events in their lives and to talk about what would have happened if these events hadn't happened. Make sure they use the third conditional.

READING AND LISTENING

1 Aim: to read for text organisation; to prepare for listening.

● As listening material this would be a difficult passage, even for students at the end of an intermediate course. So the pre-listening involves some careful reading work.

● Ask the students to do this activity on their own and then work in pairs to decide where the extracts go.

> **Answers**
> 1 a 2 d 3 i 4 e 5 g 6 c 7 j 8 h 9 b 10 f

2 Aim: to practise listening for main ideas.
- 🔊 Play the tape and ask the students to check their answers to 1.

3 Aim: to prepare for listening; to predict what is going to happen; to listen for specific information.
- Ask the students to work in pairs and to answer the questions about the next part of the story.
- 🔊 Play the tape and ask the students to listen and check.

4 Aim: to practise speaking; to practise using the third conditional.
- Ask the students to speculate about what they would have done in the circumstances, using third conditional sentences.

5 Aim: to prepare for reading.
- Ask the students to predict who does the actions and where the final meeting takes place.
- Check the answers after activity 6.

6 Aim: to read for specific information.
- Ask the students to turn to Communication activity 18 on page 102 to check their answers to activity 5.

> **Answers**
> ran out of cigarettes: Ray
> saw him waiting: the Englishman
> was beckoning him to follow: the Englishman
> called out, 'Come back here!': Ray
> ran on, faster and faster: the Englishman
> paused out of breath: Ray
> followed him to the railroad: Ray
> turned and walked away: the Englishman
> heard the Express train: Ray
>
> The final meeting takes place by the railroad tracks.

7 Aim: to practise speaking; to prepare for listening.
- Ask the students to discuss how the story might end. Who do they think the Englishman was?
- 🔊 Play the tape and ask them to listen to the end of the story.

8 Aim: to understand the writer's style.
- Ask the students if they appreciated how they think the style contributed to the tension.

VOCABULARY AND WRITING

1 Aim: to present the words in the box.
- The words are all suitable to be learnt by the students at this level, and all come from the story. Make sure everyone understands what they mean. Are there other words that are new and useful?

2 Aim: to practise writing an account of an incident.
- Ask the students to write the story from the point of view of one of the other characters. Encourage them to add as much background detail as possible.

Progress check Lessons 36–40

GENERAL COMMENTS

You can work through this Progress check in the order shown, or concentrate on areas which may have caused difficulty in Lesson 36 to 40. You can also let the students choose the activities they would like to or feel the need to do.

VOCABULARY

1 Aim: to present some common idiomatic and colloquial expressions.

● It's important to stress that the students don't necessarily have to learn these expressions to use them, only to recognise them. Encourage them to think about similar expressions in their own language which would cause foreigners difficulties.

> **Answers**
> She's all fingers and thumbs. = She's very clumsy.
> We don't see eye to eye. = We don't agree.
> He's very nosy. = He likes to know what other people are doing.
> I can't make head nor tail of it. = I don't understand it.
> I've gone and put my foot in it. = I've made a mistake.
> It cost me an arm and a leg. = It was very expensive.
> I'm all ears. = I'm listening willingly.

2 Aim: to present some idiomatic expressions with *like* and *as*.

● These idiomatic expressions with *like* and *as* are useful for students to recognise, but not to use.

> **Answers**
> to work like a dog
> to sleep like a log
> to eat like a horse
> to swim like a fish
> as drunk as a lord
> as thick as two short planks (You may like to explain this means *stupid*.)
> as stubborn as a mule
> as greedy as a pig

3 Aim: to review the vocabulary presented in Lessons 36 to 40.

● You may like to suggest that the students spend some time looking through all the vocabulary boxes in *Reward* Intermediate, looking for words they have forgotten.

● Ask the students for the words they have written and write them on the board. Ask other students to explain what they mean.

GRAMMAR

1 Aim: to review the second conditional.

> **Answers**
> 1 If Paul liked sunshine, he'd go to Spain.
> 2 If Jenny worked harder, she'd get a better job.
> 3 If you spoke more slowly, you'd be easier to understand.
> 4 If we took the car, we'd get there sooner.
> 5 If Graham spoke French, he'd live in Paris.

2 Aim: to review giving advice.

> **Possible answers**
> 1 If I were you, I'd go to bed.
> 2 I think you should count to ten.
> 3 In my opinion, you ought to wear a raincoat.
> 4 If I were you, I'd go to California.
> 5 I think you should open the window.

3 Aim: to review the use of *should have*.

> **Answers**
> 1 You should have taken the train.
> 2 You should have brought summer clothes.
> 3 You should have left earlier.
> 4 She should have rung him.
> 5 He should have looked for a cheaper one.

4 Aim: to review the use of *shouldn't have*.

> **Answers**
> 1 You shouldn't have taken the coach.
> 2 You shouldn't have brought winter clothes.
> 3 You shouldn't have arrived late.
> 4 She shouldn't have forgotten his birthday.
> 5 He shouldn't have stayed there.

5 Aim: to review the use of *might have* and *could have*.

> **Answers**
> 1 It might have been delayed.
> 2 She could have missed it.
> 3 They might have lost her baggage.
> 4 She could have come out of another exit.
> 5 We might not have seen her as she came out.

6 Aim: to review the use of *must have* and *can't have*.

> **Answers**
> 1 It must have got lost in the post.
> 2 The bus must have left already.
> 3 He can't have heard me.
> 4 He must have washed it.
> 5 It can't have been cheap.
> 6 It must be feeling ill.

7 Aim: to review *I wish*.

> **Answers**
> 1 I wish I had a new car.
> 2 I wish I had kept my tickets with my passport.
> 3 I wish I had more room.
> 4 I wish I hadn't failed my driving test.
> 5 I wish I had his address.

8 Aim: to review *if only*.

> **Answers**
> 1 If only I had a new car.
> 2 If only I had kept my tickets with my passport.
> 3 If only I had more room.
> 4 If only I hadn't failed my driving test.
> 5 If only I had his address.

9 Aim: to review the third conditional.

1 If I hadn't taken a taxi, I wouldn't have arrived in time.
2 If she hadn't spoken to him in French, they wouldn't have got on so well.
3 If he hadn't apologised, I would have lost my temper with him.
4 If we had had some money, we would have gone to the theatre.
5 If he hadn't bought a bicycle, he wouldn't have got fit.
6 If it hadn't rained all week, we would have had a good holiday.

SOUNDS

1 Aim: to focus on the different ways of pronouncing the letter *u*.
● Ask the students to say the words aloud and then group the words according to the pronunciation of the letter *u*.

> **Answers**
> /juː/: computer, junior, usual, student
> /ʌ/: funny, butter, sun
> /ɜː/: nurse, surgeon
> /ʊə/: cure, jury
> /uː/: rural

2 Aim: to focus on silent letters.
● Ask the students to underline the silent letters.

● ▭ Play the tape and ask them to listen and check.

> **Answers**
> hi<u>gh</u>li<u>gh</u>t, t<u>h</u>rou<u>gh</u>out, <u>k</u>nown, bou<u>gh</u>t, <u>Ch</u>ristian, w<u>h</u>eel, i<u>r</u>oning, ei<u>gh</u>t, <u>p</u>sy<u>ch</u>iatry

● Ask them to say the words aloud.

3 Aim: to focus on words stressed in a sentence.
● Ask the students to predict which words are likely to be stressed.

● Play the tape and ask the students to listen and check.

> **Answers**
> 1 If I'd <u>done</u> it, I'd have <u>told</u> you.
> 2 If <u>only</u> he was an <u>accountant</u>.
> 3 I <u>wish</u> I hadn't <u>eaten</u> so much.
> 4 She should have <u>asked</u> you <u>first</u>.
> 5 If I were <u>you</u>, I'd do it <u>myself</u>.
> 6 He <u>must</u> have <u>opened</u> it.

● Ask the students to say the sentences aloud.

READING AND SPEAKING

1 Aim: to read for text organisation.
● Explain that the two stories have been mixed up. Ask the students to write one of them out in full. The sentences are in the right order.

> **Answers**
> A man was saving for a new car. It was to be a surprise, and he didn't tell his wife that he had already saved £500 and hidden it in a pile of old clothes. He was out when the dustmen called and his wife gave them the old clothes. When he discovered the mistake he hired a mechanical digger to search the rubbish dump. After two days' search he gave up and started saving again.
>
> A man had worn a hearing aid for 20 years, but it had never seemed to help him hear better. When he went to hospital for a routine check-up, he was told he was wearing it in the wrong ear. He said, 'They must have made a mistake when they first gave it to me. I always thought it was useless.'

2 Aim: to practise writing; to review modal + past infinitives and *wish*.
● Ask the students to read between the lines and write sentences using the prompts.

Wordlist

The first number after each word shows the lesson in which the word first appears in the vocabulary box.
The numbers in italics show the later lessons in which the word appears again.

able /'eɪb(ə)l/ PC 11-15
accelerator /ək'selə,reɪtə(r)/ 32
accommodation
  /ə,kɒmə'deɪʃ(ə)n/ 37
accustomed /ə'kʌstəmd/ PC 11-15
acquaintance /ə'kweɪnt(ə)ns/ 36
action film /'ækʃ(ə)n fɪlm/ 21
activity /æk'tɪvɪtɪ/ 1
address /ə'dres/ 1
address book /ə'dres bʊk/ 31
adore /ə'dɔː(r)/ 25
advertisement /əd'vɜːtɪsmənt/ 24
aerial /'eərɪəl/ 32
afford /ə'fɔːd/ 8
afraid /ə'freɪd/ PC 11-15
aggressive /ə'gresɪv/ 20, 23
air force /eə(r) fɔːs/ 12
alarm clock /ə'lɑːm klɒk/ 15, 31
alive /ə'laɪv/ PC 11-15
all right /ɔːl raɪt/ 4
allergic /ə'lɜːdʒɪk/ PC 11-15
alone /ə'ləʊn/ PC 11-15
aloud /ə'laʊd/ 1
amazing /ə'meɪzɪŋ/ 21
ambition /æm'bɪʃ(ə)n/ 6
amusing /ə'mjuːzɪŋ/ 5
angry /'æŋgrɪ/ PC 11-15, 23
announcement /ə'naʊnsmənt/ 2
answer /'ɑːnsə(r)/ 1
antique /æn'tiːk/ 15
antique shop /æn'tiːk ʃɒp/ 25
apart /ə'pɑːt/ PC 11-15
appalling /ə'pɔːlɪŋ/ 21
appear /ə'pɪə(r)/ 13
apple /'æp(ə)l/ 23
appreciate /ə'priːʃɪ,eɪt/ 34
armchair /'ɑːm'tʃeə(r)/ 15, 29
army /'ɑːmɪ/ 12
aroma /ə'rəʊmə/ 33
arrival /ə'raɪv(ə)l/ 2
art gallery /'ɑːt gælərɪ/ 14
art /ɑːt/ 39
article /'ɑːtɪk(ə)l/ 24
ash /æʃ/ 33
ashtray /'æʃtreɪ/ 15
ask /ɑːsk/ 1
ask somebody out
  /ɑːsk 'sʌmbədɪ aʊt/ 36
assertive /ə'sɜːtɪv/ 20
assume /ə'sjuːm/ 38
astonished /ə'stɒnɪʃt/ PC 6-10
athlete /'æθliːt/ 30
athletics /æθ'letɪks/ 30
attack /ə'tæk/ 12
autumn /'ɔːtəm/ 37
avocado /ævə'kɑːdəʊ/ 26
avoid /ə'vɔɪd/ 34
awful /'ɔːfl/ 4
awkward /'ɔːkwəd/ 21

backpack /'bækpæk/ 19
baggage /'bægɪdʒ/ 2
bags /bægz/ 7
bake /beɪk/ 26
ballpoint pen /bɔːlpɔɪnt pen/ 31
bamboo basket
  /bæm'buː bɑːskɪt/ 37
banana /bə'nɑːnə/ 8
bananas /bə'nɑːnəz/ 28

bandage /'bændɪdʒ/ 38
bank worker /'bæŋk 'wɜːkə(r)/ 18
bar /bɑː(r)/ 9
baseball /'beɪsbɔːl/ 13
baseball cap /'beɪsbɔːl kæp/ 16
basket /'bɑːskɪt/ 30, 33
basketball /'bɑːskɪtbɔːl/ 30
bath /bɑːθ/ 29
battle /'bæt(ə)l/ 12
be born /biː bɔːn/ 1
beach /biːtʃ/ 27
bean /biːn/ 9
beans /biːnz/ 26
bear (n) /beə(r)/ 22
beard /bɪəd/ 16
beat /biːt/ 40
beautiful /'bjuːtɪfl/ 17
beer /bɪə(r)/ 28
beetroot /'biːtruːt/ 8
beige /beɪʒ/ 16
bell /bel/ 25
belt /belt/ 16
best man /best mæn/ 3
bias /'baɪəs/ 24
bicycle /'baɪsɪkl/ 15, 19
bikini /bɪ'kiːnɪ/ 16, 37
binoculars /brnɒkjʊləz/ 31
bird-watching /'bɜːdwɒtʃɪŋ/ 4
birthday /'bɜːθdeɪ/ 1
bitter /'bɪtə(r)/ 8, 9
blanket /'blæŋkɪt/ 33
blocked /blɒkt/ 29
blow up /bləʊ ʌp/ PC 21-25
blues /bluːz/ 5
boarding school /'bɔːdɪŋ skuːl/ 39
boil /bɔɪl/ 26
boiling water /'bɔɪlɪŋ 'wɔːtə(r)/ 33
bomb /bɒm/ 12
bonnet /'bɒnɪt/ 32
booking office /'bʊkɪŋ ɒfɪs/ 2
boot /buːt/ 25, 32
boots /buːts/ 30
border /'bɔːdə(r)/ 12
bored /bɔːd/ PC 11-15
boring /'bɔːrɪŋ/ 4, 5
bow tie /bəʊ taɪ/ 16
bowl /bəʊl/ 26
box /bɒks/ 25
boxer /'bɒksə(r)/ 30
boxer shorts /'bɒksə(r) ʃɔːts/ 16
boxing /'bɒksɪŋ/ 30
boyfriend /'bɔɪfrend/ 36
brake /breɪk/ 32
brake light /breɪk laɪt/ 32
bread /bred/ 8
break up /breɪk ʌp/ 36
bride /braɪd/ 3
bridesmaid /'braɪdzmeɪd/ 3
bridge /brɪdʒ/ 14
bright /braɪt/ 33
brilliant /'brɪlɪənt/ 4
broadcast /'brɔːdkɑːst/ 24
broadsheet /'brɔːdʃiːt/ 24
broken /'brəʊkən/ 29
brother /'brʌðə(r)/ 1
brush /brʌʃ/ 17
brush off /brʌʃ ɒf/ 33
build /bɪld/ 28
builder /'bɪldə(r)/ 29

bullet /'bʊlɪt/ 12
bumper /'bʌmpə(r)/ 32
bunch /bʌntʃ/ 10
burst /bɜːst/ 29
business card /'bɪznɪs kɑːd/ 31
busy /'bɪzɪ/ 11, 14
butter /'bʌtə(r)/ 9
butterfly /'bʌtəflaɪ/ 22
buy /baɪ/ 7, 11

cab /kæb/ 2
cab rank /kæb ræŋk/ 2
cabbage /'kæbɪdʒ/ 8
cake /keɪk/ 3
canal /kə'næl/ 27
canary /kə'neərɪ/ 16
cancel /'kæns(ə)l/ 2
canvas /'kænvəs/ 16
capable /'keɪpəb(ə)l/ PC 11-15
capture /'kæptʃə(r)/ 35
car horn /kɑː hɔːn/ 2
car repair /'kɑː rɪ'peə(r)/ 39
cardigan /'kɑːdɪgən/ 16
carpenter /'kɑːpɪntə(r)/ 29
carpet /'kɑːpɪt/ 29, 33
carry /'kærɪ/ 7
cars /kɑːz/ 28
cartoon /kɑː'tuːn/ 13
cash /'kæʃ/ 3, 31
casserole /'kæsə,rəʊl/ 26
cassette player /kə'set 'pleɪə(r)/ 32
castle /'kɑːs(ə)l/ 14
casual /'kæʒʊəl/ 10
casually /'kæʒʊəlɪ/ 40
catch /kætʃ/ 2
catch up with
  /kætʃ ʌp wɪθ/ PC 21-25
cathedral /kə'θiːdrəl/ 14, 19
cause /kɔːz/ 34
ceiling /'siːlɪŋ/ 29
cemetery /'semətrɪ/ 14
ceremony /'serɪmənɪ/ 3
certain /'sɜːt(ə)n/ PC 11-15
channel /'tʃæn(ə)l/ 24
charming /'tʃɑːmɪŋ/ 21
chart /tʃɑːt/ 1
chat show /'tʃæt ʃəʊ/ 24
chatter /'tʃætə(r)/ 38
check /tʃek/ 1
chemical /'kemɪk(ə)l/ 9
chemistry /'kemɪstrɪ/ 39
cheque book /tʃek bʊk/ 31
chewing gum /'tʃuːɪŋ gʌm/ 33
children /'tʃɪldrən/ 1
chilly /'tʃɪlɪ/ 8
china /'tʃaɪnə/ 15, 28
chocolate /'tʃɒklət/ 16, 31
chop /tʃɒp/ 26
Christian /'krɪstɪən/ 3
chrysanthemum
  /krɪ'sænθəməm/ 23
church /tʃɜːtʃ/ 3, 19
circle /'sɜːk(ə)l/ 1
circulation /sɜːkjʊ'leɪʃ(ə)n/ 24
classical /'klæsɪk(ə)l/ 5
clean /kliːn/ 11, 29
clock /klɒk/ 33
cloth /klɒθ/ 28
club /klʌb/ 12

clue /kluː/ 38
clumsy /'klʌmzɪ/ 21
clutch /klʌtʃ/ 32
coach /kəʊtʃ/ 2
coal /kəʊl/ 28, 33
coast-to-coast /kəʊst tə kəʊst/ 35
cocoa /'kəʊkəʊ/ 9
coffee /'kɒfɪ/ 28
coffee cup /'kɒfɪ kʌp/ 15
coffee-house /'kɒfɪ haʊs/ 14
cold /kəʊld/ 9
colleague /'kɒliːg/ 10
collect /kɒlekt/ 11
comedy /'kɒmədɪ/ 21
comic /'kɒmɪk/ 13
commercial /kə'mɜːʃ(ə)l/ 24
companion /kəm'pænɪən/ 38
compete /kəm'piːt/ 30
complain about
  /kəm'pleɪn ə'baʊt/ 7
complete /kəm'pliːt/ 1
comprehensive school
  /kɒmprɪ'hensɪv skuːl/ 39
computer studies
  /kəm'pjuːtə(r) 'stʌdɪz/ 39
computers /kəm'pjuːtəz/ 28
concert hall /'kɒnsət hɔːl/ 14
confidence /'kɒnfɪdəns/ 6
confident /'kɒnfɪdənt/ PC 11-15, 20
confused /kən'fjuːzd/ 8
connection /kə'nekʃn/ 2
consumption /kən'sʌmʃ(ə)n/ 34
conversation /kɒnvə'seɪʃn/ 1
cook /kʊk/ 26
cool /kuːl/ 20
cool-headed /kuːl hedɪd/ 20
cosmopolitan /kɒzmə'pɒlɪt(ə)n/ 14
cost /kɒst/ 7
cotton /'kɒtn/ 15, 16, 28
country and western
  /'kʌntrɪ ənd 'west(ə)n/ 5
couple /'kʌp(ə)l/ 3
court /kɔːt/ 30
cover /'kʌvə(r)/ 38
crash /kræʃ/ 35
crazy /'kreɪzɪ/ 40
cream /kriːm/ 16, 26
credit card /'kredɪt kɑːd/ 31
crew cut /kruː kʌt/ 16
cricket /'krɪkɪt/ 4
criminal /'krɪmɪn(ə)l/ 13
crimson /'krɪmz(ə)n/ 16
crisp /krɪsp/ 33
crop /krɒp/ 9
cross /krɒs/ 10
crowded /'kraʊdɪd/ 10, 14
crowds /kraʊdz/ 2, 8, 27
cruel /kruːəl/ 23
cultural /'kʌltʃərəl/ 34
currency /'kʌrənsɪ/ 12
curse /kɜːs/ 23
curtains /'kɜːtənz/ 29
customer /'kʌstəm(r)/ 10
customs /'kʌstəmz/ 27
cut /kʌt/ 26, 29
cynical /'sɪnɪk(ə)l/ 23

daily /'deɪlɪ/ 24
damage /'dæmɪdʒ/ 34

124

Progress Test 1 Lessons 1–10

SECTION 1: VOCABULARY (30 marks)

1a Underline the odd-one-out and leave a group of three related words. (10 marks)

b Add one other word to the groups of words. (10 marks)

Example: brother child <u>house</u> husband *grandmother*

1 brilliant dull superb wonderful _____

2 basketball cricket gardening tennis _____

3 ask complete story tick _____

4 blues folk singer soul _____

5 Danish English French Germany _____

6 what where while why _____

7 believe crowded love understand _____

8 afraid always never sometimes _____

9 confidence family reliability talent _____

10 customer colleague friend present _____

2 Complete these sentences with ten different adjectives. (10 marks)

Example: He's very <u>*serious*</u> . He never laughs.

1 I don't mind watching cartoons. They're _____ .

2 It's your birthday soon, isn't it? Are you _____ ?

3 Eating too many chips and crisps isn't _____ .

4 I was very _____ when I didn't know the answer. Everyone laughed at me.

5 After eating nothing all day, I felt very _____ .

6 I'm _____ . There's nothing interesting on TV.

7 Our teacher's very _____ . She always explains things again if we don't understand.

8 My surname is Pirini and my _____ name is Silvia.

9 The film had a _____ ending. Everyone died.

10 Chocolate is _____ but sausage is savoury.

Progress Test 1 Lessons 1–10

SECTION 2: GRAMMAR (30 marks)

3a Choose ten of these words to complete the first ten spaces in the conversation. (10 marks)

Example: a) are b) is c) were

1 a) buying b) doing c) looking
2 a) coming b) visiting c) going
3 a) use b) used c) would
4 a) for b) during c) since
5 a) is b) isn't c) hasn't
6 a) adore b) detest c) hate
7 a) where b) which c) who
8 a) are b) do c) were
9 a) to try b) try c) trying
10 a) can't b) don't c) wasn't

b Complete the last ten spaces with ten of your own words. (10 marks)

JONATHAN: Hello, Rebecca. What ____are____ you doing here?

REBECCA: I'm (1) _____ some shopping for my holidays. I'm (2) _____ to Majorca next week.

JONATHAN: Majorca! We (3) _____ to go there when I was young. We had an apartment (4) _____ two weeks a year. Majorca's lovely, (5) _____it?

REBECCA: Yes, it's beautiful at this time of year. Paul and I (6) _____ walking and it's good for that. The hotel, (7) _____ we are staying, is near the sea so Paul can go water-skiing.

JONATHAN: And (8) _____ you go water-skiing too? I'd love (9) _____ that.

REBECCA: No, I don't. I (10) _____ mind swimming but not water-skiing. It's too dangerous for me.

JONATHAN: I don't know Paul, (11) _____ I?

REBECCA: I don't think so. I met him (12) _____ I was on holiday in Crete last year. He (13) _____ working there.

JONATHAN: Where (14) _____ you meet him?

REBECCA: Well, he was a waiter. And I met him in the hotel bar as (15) _____ as I got there. He bought (16) _____ a drink on my first evening. I saw him (17) _____ day after that.

JONATHAN: Wow! Sounds good.

REBECCA: He's living (18) _____ London now so I see him most weekends. Why don't you come for dinner on Saturday and meet him?

JONATHAN: I'm sorry (19) _____ I can't. I'm going to a wedding on Saturday.

REBECCA: Never (20) _____ . Come round another time.

4 Rewrite these sentences. Begin with the words in brackets. (10 marks)

Example: I hate living here. (I can't)
I can't stand living here.

1 Could you open the door? (Would you)
_____

2 He got up. He had breakfast. (After)
_____

3 When she phoned, I was watching television. (While)
_____

4 Could you repeat that? (I wonder if)
_____

5 She made a cup of coffee and then opened her book. (Before)
_____

6 Saturday is the best day for me to do the shopping. (I like)
_____

7 We were having lunch when the police arrived. (As)
_____

8 Can you explain what this means? (What)
_____

9 Does it matter? (It doesn't)
_____

10 He met her last week. (She)
_____

129

Progress Test 1 Lessons 1–10

SECTION 3: READING (20 marks)

5 Read the passage *Christmas, the Japanese way.*
There are four paragraphs in the passage. Which
paragraphs describe these things? (2 marks)

   a   typical Christmas gifts

   b   a popular Japanese Christmas tradition

6 Are these sentences true (T) or false (F) or doesn't
the passage say (DS)? (10 marks)

     Example: Some Japanese people are Christian. ☐ *T*

   a   The Japanese have always celebrated Christmas. ☐

   b   In Japan there are big family meals at Christmas. ☐

   c   The fireworks display at Disneyland is very
popular. ☐

   d   Christmas boat trips last all evening. ☐

   e   Women buy more presents than men. ☐

7 Find four things, everyday and special, that the
passage says you can do in Tokyo on 25 December.
Make notes. (8 marks)

———————————————————————

———————————————————————

———————————————————————

———————————————————————

———————————————————————

———————————————————————

———————————————————————

———————————————————————

———————————————————————

———————————————————————

Christmas, the Japanese way

In principle, Christmas should not be celebrated
here, since the Japanese are mostly Buddhist or
Shintoist, and about 1% only are Christian. From
the government's point of view, 25 December is
just another working day, with offices, shops and
the stockmarket open for business. But Japan is
quick to pick up an idea from overseas. And so
department stores are full of Christmas
decorations, special 'present offers' are on sale
and traditional carols replace everyday music.

Yet, many of the traditional Christmas customs
have a strong Japanese feel. For example, instead
of the usual family meals, more and more young
couples are celebrating Christmas in a modern
way; they are spending the night of Christmas
Eve in a hotel. If money is not a problem, this
'celebration' includes champagne and the gift of
a diamond necklace.

Here are some suggestions for those who are in
Tokyo this Christmas and have nothing special
to do. The spectacular evening fireworks display
at Tokyo Disneyland takes place every year on
the 24th and 25th. Tickets are usually sold out in
November. But don't worry – you pass
Disneyland on the way to or from the airport. So,
if you're flying into the city at night, get a seat on
the left-hand side of the bus from the airport and
watch the fireworks for free from the traffic jams
on the expressway. Or you could take a
Christmas boat trip in Tokyo bay, where guests
on special boats can have a champagne and
turkey dinner as they pass the factories,
chemical refineries and warehouses. A two-hour
cruise on the *Vingt et Un* boat, including dinner
and a Christmas present, is £312 for two.

Present-giving in Japan is a way of life. And this is
true for Christmas too. According to a
spokesman for Marui department store, the
average price of a present from a woman to a
man is £106. Women, on the other hand, are
receiving more expensive gifts, on average £193.
Men like to receive clothes, watches and ties and
jewellery is popular with women. The giving of
presents at Christmas is something that the
Japanese do better than those of us in the west!

Adapted from *Christmas for everyone*
by Terry McCarthy, *Independent on Sunday*

Photocopiable

Progress Test 1 Lessons 1–10

SECTION 4: WRITING (20 marks)

8 Write a letter to a friend. Describe a trip you made or a special event
you went to recently. Write 15 to 20 sentences. (20 marks)

Photocopiable

Progress Test 2 Lessons 11–20

SECTION 1: VOCABULARY (30 marks)

1 Match the ten words in the list with ten words from the box. (10 marks)

1 air 2 alarm 3 art 4 bow 5 coffee 6 common

7 concert 8 crew 9 fountain 10 prime

> bag brush car clock cup cut fire force
>
> gallery hall house mail minister pen
>
> present sense shorts table tie tray

2 Find ten adjectives in the box below which usually go after a noun. (10 marks)

> afraid alive antique apart bored confident
>
> few funny glad hard ill lovely practical
>
> proud ready sorry sure typical unable well

_____   _____

_____   _____

_____   _____

_____   _____

_____   _____

3 Complete these sentences with ten different particles. (10 marks)

Example: He took _out_ his camera and took a photo.

1 Please bring the book _____ when you finish it.

2 She gave her old clothes _____ because she didn't need them.

3 Would you mind filling _____ this form?

4 I'm looking _____ my cardigan. Have you seen it?

5 They called _____ the football match because of the bad weather.

6 Have you tidied _____ your things in the bathroom?

7 I never get _____ with things I have to do.

8 Can you look _____ the children while I'm at work?

9 Can you turn the heating _____ ? It's very hot.

10 I'm going to go _____ the documents again.

Progress Test 2 Lessons 11–20

SECTION 2: GRAMMAR (30 marks)

4a Choose ten of these words to complete the first ten spaces in the passage. (10 marks)

Example: a) are you b) <u>have you been</u> c) were you

1   a) didn't write b) have written c) haven't written

2   a) age b) ago c) old

3   a) during b) for c) since

4   a) has b) should c) supposed

5   a) can b) can't c) must

6   a) can b) can't c) must

7   a) hers b) his c) theirs

8   a) going b) going to c) want

9   a) as b) in c) than

10   a) many b) more c) much

b Complete the last ten spaces with ten of your own words. (10 marks)

5 Rewrite these sentences. Begin with the words in brackets. (10 marks)

Example: Paris is as beautiful as Rome. (Rome)
Rome is as beautiful as Paris.

1   In Sydney there are more people than in Perth. (In Perth)
_____

2   Florida is more dangerous than Texas. (Texas)
_____

3   You have to wear uniform. (You're)
_____

4   Am I supposed to use the fax? (Should)
_____

5   Germany has fewer tourists than France. (France)
_____

6   Rome is bigger than Milan. (Milan)
_____

7   It's possible that I'll be away. (I)
_____

8   You can't smoke here. (You're not)
_____

9   I'm certain he'll write. (He's certain)
_____

10   We haven't bought a television yet. (We still)
_____

---

8 Riverside, Oxford, OX2 7HJ

December 8th

Dear Keith,

How are you? What *have you been* doing recently? I'm sorry I (1) _____ for a long time.

I moved away from Torbay eight months (2) _____ . I've been working in Oxford (3) _____ September. I'm working as a receptionist in a computer company. It's (4) _____ to be one of the biggest in the country. I think it (5) _____ be - we've got a lot of customers and I'm always very busy. The work (6) _____ be quite tiring.

I'm staying with Lucia, a girl from work, at the moment. The house used to be her parents but it's (7) _____ now. I'm (8) _____ buy my own flat. Flats are more expensive in Oxford (9) _____ in Torbay and I haven't got as (10) _____ money as I need. I (11) _____ looked at about twenty - but I haven't found the right one (12) _____ . But I'm (13) _____ looking! I'm (14) _____ I'll find one soon!

Have you (15) _____ been to Oxford? It's famous (16) _____ its university but there are lots of other things I like about it. There's one thing I prefer about Torbay - Oxford has (17) _____ rain. I wanted to go for a walk yesterday but it was raining so I wasn't (18) _____ to go out. You (19) _____ to have an umbrella here! In fact, it looks as (20) _____ it's going to rain again!

I'll stop now. Please write and tell me your news.

Love
Isobel

133

Photocopiable

Progress Test 2   Lessons 11–20

SECTION 3: READING (20 marks)

6 Read the passage *Coffee, Italian-style*.
Was Tim Parks on holiday when he visited
the bar? Or was he living in Italy? (2 marks)

_____

_____

7 Imagine that you are moving to Italy to live.
Does Tim Parks advise you to do these things in
an Italian bar?
Put a tick (✓) by the things he advises you to do
and a cross (✗) by the things you shouldn't do.
(4 marks)

1 eat pastries before ten-thirty in the morning

2 ask for long-life milk in your coffee

3 put wine in your coffee

4 only drink cappuccino before lunch

8 Are these sentences true (T) or false (F) or
doesn't the passage say (DS)? (6 marks)

Example: Montecchio is a large town. ☐F☐

1 The Pasticceria Maggia is the only bar in
   Montecchio. ☐

2 Only bars in the country serve *grappa*. ☐

3 In some bars you pay before you order. ☐

4 Tim Parks doesn't like going to business or
   tourist bars. ☐

5 Tim Parks and his wife arrived in Montecchio on
   a Sunday. ☐

6 Tim Parks' wife is Italian. ☐

9 Why does Tim Parks like the Pasticceria Maggia
so much? Write four sentences giving your
reasons. (8 marks)

_____

_____

_____

_____

_____

_____

_____

Coffee, Italian-style

The morning after our arrival in Montecchio, we set off to try the village bars. And for anyone moving to Italy, this is a habit that I would very much recommend.

Timing is very important. If you want to order milky coffee and a pastry, cappuccino and brioche, you should arrive before ten-thirty. Of course, you could order the same things later in the day but this would show that you are foreign. Italians usually like foreign visitors. But they like foreigners more if they agree that the Italian way of doing things is best. When a tourist orders a cappuccino rather than an espresso after lunch, they smile to themselves. Imagine pouring all that milk onto an already full stomach!

Note this warning. If the first taste of your cappuccino tells you that the milk is of the long-life variety, change bar before you spend too much time there. Either the bar is very much out in the country where nobody appreciates cappuccino, or this is a bar where most people are ordering wine or grappa. If they are ordering coffee, they are putting wine or grappa, but definitely not milk, in it.

Avoid bars where you have to pay before you order your drink. If you want to sit down in such bars, you will have to pay for waiter service. So, you will have to pay extra if you pick up your coffee and sit down with it. More important, these are not bars where the same people come and relax every day. No, these are busy bars, business bars, tourist bars. I do not recommend them.

My wife and I went to the Pasticceria Maggia, our local cake shop and bar, that very first Sunday. We ordered at the bar from the girl who was serving. I picked up my cappuccino and brioche and settled into a comfortable chair. My coffee was delicious! I picked up the Gazzetto dello Sport and studied the English football results! (Every bar in Italy is obliged to buy newspapers for its customers.) The whole experience was so relaxing. We have been regular customers since that very first visit.

I have lived in London, Cambridge, Boston. I have spent long periods of time in Switzerland and New York and have holidayed in most of Western Europe. I can honestly say that the Pasticceria Maggia is the most pleasant place for the ordering and drinking of coffee.

Adapted from *Italian neighbours* by Tim Parks

Progress Test 2 Lessons 11–20

SECTION 4: WRITING (20 marks)

10 Write about your job or your life at school. Describe what you do every day.
Try to write about some of your experiences and your plans. Write 15 to 20 sentences.

_____

_____

_____

_____

_____

_____

_____

_____

_____

_____

_____

_____

_____

_____

_____

_____

_____

_____

_____

_____

_____

Progress Test 3 Lessons 21–30

SECTION 1: VOCABULARY (30 marks)

1a Underline the odd-one-out and leave a group of three related words. (5 marks)

b Add one other word to the groups of words. (5 marks)

Example: avocado pepper turkey wine *fish*

1 musical sitcom thriller western _____

2 jaguar leopard moose vulture _____

3 boil fry peel roast _____

4 builder carpenter electrician

   replaster _____

5 distillery factory mill pottery _____

2 Complete the sentences with one of the words in brackets. (10 marks)

Example: Come and *look* at this. (look/watch)

1 Can you _____ me some money?

   (borrow/lend)

2 Please _____ me my diary. (bring/lend)

3 Can you _____ the table? (lay/lie)

4 I've _____ my briefcase at home.

   (forgotten/left)

5 You haven't _____ any mistakes.

   (done/made)

6 Where did you _____ these apples? (buy/sell)

7 I'm _____ my exam results very soon.

   (expecting/waiting)

8 I didn't _____ television last night.

   (see/watch)

9 When did you _____ your handbag?

   (loose/lose)

10 Passports are always _____ at the airport.

   (checked/controlled)

3 Complete the sentences with ten different verbs. (10 marks)

Example: __*Cut*__ the onion with a sharp knife.

1 Could you _____ me your pen?

2 If we don't take a map, we may _____

   our way.

3 Can you _____ this sink? It's filthy.

4 How many goals did your team _____ ?

5 Why don't you leave now? I'll _____ up

   with you.

6 Milk can _____ off if you leave it in the sun.

7 The shower isn't working. I'll get a plumber to

   _____ it.

8 Then _____ the mixture over the bottom of

   the pan.

9 I'm going to _____ down on my bed.

10 I'll _____ for Susan. She'll be here soon.

Progress Test 3: Lessons 21–30

SECTION 2: GRAMMAR (30 marks)

4a Choose ten of these words to complete the first ten spaces in the letter. (10 marks)

Example: a) bought
b) <u>moved</u> c) went

1 a) wanted b) will

   c) would

2 a) do b) have c) make

3 a) as b) than c) that

4 a) excite b) excited

   c) exciting

5 a) mend b) to mend

   c) to be mended

6 a) promised

   b) suggested c) warned

7 a) her b) him c) them

8 a) is b) has c) has been

9 a) me b) my c) myself

10 a) I b) I'll c) I'm

---

27 Godstow Road
Oxford

Dear Keith

Thank you for your letter. I have just <u>moved</u> into my new home. I said I (1) _____ send you my new address so (2) _____ sure you come and see me!

As far (3) _____ I am concerned, it's the nicest house I've seen - I am extremely (4) _____ about it! A builder looked at it last week and said that the windows needed (5) _____ . He (6) _____ that I replace them. I think I'll have (7) _____ do that before the winter. The garden (8) _____ overgrown too. I can do most of the gardening (9) _____ . If it's too much work, perhaps (10) _____ get a gardener to help me.

On Saturday Peter phoned. (Peter's the friend (11) _____ knows my sister.) He asked (12) _____ I was busy. I (13) _____ him that I was only putting my things in boxes! He easily persuaded (14) _____ to go to Blenheim Palace, (15) _____ is just north of Oxford.

Blenheim was well worth (16) _____ . While we were there, we saw the bedroom (17) _____ Winston Churchill was born. The palace (18) _____ built in the eighteenth century. It's a lovely building. The gardens (19) _____ designed by Capability Brown - it was pleasant (20) _____ walk round them after visiting the house.

I hope you can come and see me soon.

Love
Isobel

---

b Complete the last ten spaces with ten of your own words. (10 marks)

5 Rewrite these sentences. Begin with the words in brackets. (10 marks)

Example: I stopped smoking a year ago. (I gave)
I gave up smoking a year ago.

1 My uncle drives appallingly. (My uncle is)

   _____

2 'I saw a lion yesterday,' he said. (He said he)

   _____

3 'Are soap operas the most popular programmes?' he asked. (He asked)

   _____

4 'Be careful,' she said to her son. (She warned)

   _____

5 The best film I've ever seen is *The Piano*. (*The Piano*)

   _____

6 'I'll marry you, I promise,' she said. (She promised)

   _____

7 People play football all over the world. (Football)

   _____

8 She said she couldn't find a saucepan. ('I)

   _____

9 I'll ask the shop assistant to wrap up the present. (I'll have)

   _____

10 I have quite a good relationship with my parents. (I get)

   _____

Photocopiable

Progress Test 3   Lessons 21–30

SECTION 3: READING
(20 marks)

6   Read *Eat your heart out ... in Australia*. Does the article say if Australian food is getting better or worse? Why? Find two reasons in the passage.
(4 marks)

_____

_____

7   Are these sentences true (T) or false (F) or doesn't the passage say (DS)?
(8 marks)

Example: Australians eat out a lot. [T]

1   The writer does not like pie floater. ☐

2   Meat is often served in pubs. ☐

3   The best way to cook kangaroo is to grill it. ☐

4   The writer has not tried witjuti grubs. ☐

5   Seafood is as cheap as meat in Australia. ☐

6   Not many exotic vegetables are available. ☐

7   Bananas are grown in Tasmania. ☐

8   The writer thinks that Lamington is delicious. ☐

8   The passage says that *Australia is almost two nations when it comes to food*. What are the two nations? Write sentences about the food that is typical of these nations. (8 marks)

_____

_____

_____

_____

_____

_____

Eat your heart out ... in Australia

Australia is almost two separate nations when it comes to food. In the cities of the southeast – especially Melbourne – there's a range of fantastic, international and, above all, inexpensive restaurants and cafés with almost every imaginable cuisine. Here there is an exceptionally high number of eating places. These restaurants survive because people eat out so much – three times a week is not unusual. Remote country areas are the complete opposite of this; microwavable fast-food and meat pies are the most common items on offer. If you're in Queensland or South Australia, ask for a pie floater, an upside-down meat pie, which floats in peas and tomato sauce. Ordinary pies are bad enough – when you find this speciality, you may ask yourself if it was worth looking for!

Traditionally, Australian food has been awful. But two things have rescued the country from its poor diet: immigration, and an amazing range of superb, fresh, locally-produced ingredients. Immigrants have not only brought their own food customs with them; they have also had an effect on Australian food. As a result 'modern Australian' cuisine is an exciting mix of traditional and modern tastes with influences from around the world – particularly Asia and the Mediterranean.

Meat is plentiful, cheap and excellent. It is an important part of the pub meal and of the 'barbie' or barbecue, the most Australian of eating habits. Free or coin-operated electric barbecues can be found in car parks and campgrounds all over the country. As well as beef and lamb, you may also find more exotic meats, especially in more upmarket restaurants, such as emu, buffalo and camel. But the two most common are kangaroo, which is very tough if overcooked but deliciously tender if served properly, and crocodile, which tastes like a mixture of chicken and pork, and is best grilled. If you're feeling adventurous, try witjuti grubs – eating these caterpillars live is traditional, but it might be better to try them roasted. Either way, they are said to taste like peanuts. At the coast, and at specialist restaurants, there's tremendous seafood too – including prawns, oysters and lobsters. The choice of vegetables is predictable – beans, carrots, potatoes etc – but again, they'll be fresh, cheap and good.

Fruit is good too, from Tasmanian apples and pears to tropical bananas, mangoes, avocados, pineapples and coconuts. If it's desserts you're interested in, then try the two Australian specialities. Pavlova, or pav, is named after the famous Russian ballerina and consists of meringue, fruit and cream. Lamington, which is less interesting than its name suggests, is a chocolate sponge cake, covered in coconut.

Vegetarians might think that they will have a narrow choice of food in Australia – and in the country areas that's probably true. But elsewhere most restaurants have one vegetarian choice at least, and in the cities vegetarian cafés have a healthy, image which suits Australians' active, health-conscious nature.

Adapted from *The Rough Guide to Australia* published by Rough Guides Ltd

Progress Test 3 Lessons 21–30

SECTION 4: WRITING (20 marks)

9 Think about a film or TV programme you have seen or a book your have read recently.
   Describe what happened. Try to use a variety of different structures. Write 15 to 20 sentences. (20 marks)

Photocopiable

Progress Test 4 Lessons 31–40

SECTION 1: VOCABULARY (30 marks)

1 Match the ten words in the list with ten words from the box. (10 marks)

1 ballpoint 2 credit 3 cheque 4 chewing 5 ice

6 gear 7 mobile 8 olive 9 physical 10 state

> board book brush card clock cube friend
> gauge gum high lever oil pen phone
> education player repair repellent school
> wheel

2 Underline the word which usually goes first in these pairs. (10 marks)

Example: eggs <u>bacon</u>

1 bread cheese

2 pepper salt

3 fork knife

4 apples pears

5 chips fish

6 oil vinegar

7 cup saucer

8 bread butter

9 cream strawberries

10 milk sugar

3 Complete these sentences with ten different nouns. (10 marks)

Example: This coffee has lost its _aroma_ .

1 I opened the _____ of the car and looked at

the engine.

2 My younger brother swims like a _____ .

3 There's a spectacular _____ from the roof of

the hotel.

4 I've cut my finger. Can you put a _____ on it?

5 Can you pass the salt and _____ , please?

6 I usually sleep like a _____ .

7 Let's take the _____ to the fourth floor.

8 Do you take milk and _____ with your tea?

9 I can't make _____ nor tail of it.

10 A _____ is a young dog.

SECTION 2: GRAMMAR (30 marks)

4a Choose ten of these words to complete the first ten spaces in the passage. (10 marks)

Example: a) <u>matter</u> b) news c) wrong

1 a) I fall b) I'm falling c) I've fallen

2 a) did b) does c) will

3 a) meet b) saw c) spoke

4 a) finishes b) has finished c) had finished

5 a) won't have b) wouldn't c) wouldn't have

6 a) looks b) smiles c) talks

7 a) hasn't b) isn't c) wasn't

8 a) had been sitting b) had sat c) sat

9 a) do b) done c) have done

10 a) had spoken b) speak c) spoke

© Reed Educational & Professional Publishing Limited 1995. This sheet may be photocopied for use in class.

Progress Test 4 Lessons 31–40

b Complete the last ten spaces with ten of your own words. (10 marks)

JONATHAN: Hello, Rebecca. What's the _matter_ ?

REBECCA: (1) _____ out with Paul.

JONATHAN: Paul? Your boyfriend? When

(2) _____ this happen?

REBECCA: On Friday. We were having a pizza when he

(3) _____ an old girlfriend. After he

(4) _____ his meal, he got up and

went to speak to her. If he wasn't so

attractive, I (5) _____ worry so much.

But I always feel awful if he (6) _____

to another woman. I wish I (7) _____

so jealous. But I (8) _____ on my own

for about ten minutes when he came back.

Then I just left the restaurant – on my own.

JONATHAN: What would you (9) _____ if he had

followed you?

REBECCA: I don't know. But I wish I (10) _____

to him.

JONATHAN: Why don't you phone him (11) _____

tell him how you feel? I think you

(12) _____ to say something. You

(13) _____ have walked out of the

restaurant on Friday.

REBECCA: You're probably right. I'll phone him as

(14) _____ as I get home. After all,

I (15) _____ be very upset if we broke

up.

JONATHAN: What will you do if he (16) _____

want to see you again?

REBECCA: I don't know. I'll have to think of something

in (17) _____ that happens. He

(18) _____ have already decided not

to see me again.

JONATHAN: Well, phone me after you (19) _____

spoken to him. I'm (20) _____ to be

at home all evening.

REBECCA: Thanks a lot, Jonathan.

5 Rewrite these sentences. Begin with the words in brackets. (10 marks)

Example: You should lose some weight. (You ought)
You ought to lose some weight.

1 I didn't work very hard for my exams. (I wish)

_____

2 Perhaps she phoned when we were out. (She might)

_____

3 Perhaps I have left my watch at home. (I could)

_____

4 Sally is likely to be late. (Sally will)

_____

5 To keep fit and healthy, take lots of exercise. (By)

_____

6 I went out with him for several months, then we got married. (After)

_____

7 I'll take a drink in case I get thirsty. (I might)

_____

8 Call a taxi and you won't miss your train. (If you)

_____

9 It was wrong of me not to leave a tip. (I should)

_____

10 I'd love to live in a big house. (I wish)

_____

Photocopiable

Progress Test 4 Lessons 31–40

SECTION 3: READING (20 marks)

6 Read the passage and choose the best title. (2 marks)

a A case of mistaken identity.

b Who killed Sandra Rivett?

c The case of the disappearing Earl.

7 When exactly did Sandra Rivett die? (2 marks)

_____day _____ber____th, 19_____

8 Are these sentences true (T) or false (F) or doesn't the passage say (DS)? (8 marks)

Example: Both the Lucans liked gambling. |DS|

a The Lucans shared the same house. ☐

b They had three children. ☐

c Lucan phoned his mother twice on the night of the murder. ☐

d The nanny had gone downstairs to meet someone. ☐

e Susan Maxwell Scott was one of Lucan's gambling friends. ☐

f He drove to her house in his own car. ☐

g He made some phone calls from Mrs Maxwell Scott's house. ☐

h He stayed overnight at her house. ☐

9 Lucan's friends called him 'Lucky'. Why do you think they did this? But was he really lucky? Write four sentences giving your reasons. (8 marks)

_____

_____

_____

_____

It was a wet night in early November 1974 when Lady Veronica Lucan ran into The Plumbers' Arms. With blood pouring from her head, she burst into the pub shouting: 'Help me … I've just escaped from a murderer … he's in the house … he's murdered the nanny.' The man she referred to was the Earl of Lucan, a gambling aristocrat known as 'Lucky' and Lady Lucan's ex-husband. The police were called and entered Lady Lucan's home, an expensive Georgian house in Belgravia.

The house was dark. But when Sergeant Donald Baker shone his torch down the hallway, he noticed bloodstains on the walls. At the bottom of the stairs, he discovered the body of the children's nanny, Sandra Rivett, and the murder weapon, a lead pipe.

Soon Lucan's mother arrived at the house. She said that her son had just phoned and asked her to go there. He had told his mother that there had been a 'terrible catastrophe' and that Veronica and the nanny were injured. He had asked her to collect the children from the house. Just before midnight Lucan again called. 'I will ring the police in the morning,' he told her. He never phoned the police.

At first, Roy Ranson, head of the investigation, had no reason to think that Lucan was the murderer. But Lady Lucan, who had gone downstairs after the nanny and been attacked herself, had no doubt that the attacker was her ex-husband. She thought that he had killed the nanny by mistake. Sandra's night off each week was Thursday, but that week she had taken Wednesday off instead. Perhaps Sandra's killer had gone to the house expecting only Lady Lucan to be there.

Susan Maxwell Scott, a friend of Lucan's, was the last person to have seen Lucan alive. He arrived at her house towards midnight on the night of the murder. Lucan told her that he had been passing his wife's home, on his way to his own flat, when he had seen a man attacking her. Lucan had entered the house using his key and the man had run off. Mrs Maxwell Scott told police that Lucan drove off at about 1.15 am after writing letters to two friends.

On Sunday 10 November the police at Newhaven, on the south coast, found the car used by Lord Lucan. There was blood inside the car and also some lead pipe, identical to the murder weapon, in the boot. These did not belong to the car's owner, a friend who had lent it to Lucan two weeks earlier.

So, what happened to Lucan? Did he escape to Europe and then perhaps to Africa? Or did he jump into the sea and end his life? Did he murder Sandra Rivett? Did he murder her by mistake? Or did he pay someone to kill his wife? Perhaps we will never know. A jury found Lucan, in his absence, guilty of murder and his mysterious behaviour perhaps confirms this view, yet he has never been found. The police file on the case is still open and the mystery of 'Lucky' Lucan remains.

Adapted from *Unsolved cases*, published for St Michael by Macdonald & Co (Publishers) Ltd

Progress Test 4 Lessons 31–40

SECTION 4: WRITING (20 marks)

10 You recently bought a piece of electrical equipment, eg a fax machine, an alarm clock, and you are not satisfied with it. Write a letter of complaint. Say what is wrong with the piece of equipment and what you would like to happen. Remember to use the layout and forms appropriate for a letter of complaint.

_____

_____

_____

_____

_____

_____

_____

_____

_____

_____

_____

_____

_____

_____

_____

_____

_____

_____

_____

_____

_____

_____

Answers Progress Test 1 Lessons 1–10

SECTION 1: VOCABULARY [30 marks]

1a (10 marks: 1 mark for each correct answer.)

1	dull	6	while
2	gardening	7	crowded
3	story	8	afraid
4	singer	9	family
5	Germany	10	present

b (10 marks: 1 mark for each appropriate answer.)

1 an adjective with a positive meaning, eg *great*
2 a sport, eg *swimming*
3 a verb used in instructions, eg *read*
4 a type of music, eg *opera*
5 a nationality adjective, eg *Chinese*
6 a question word, eg *when*
7 a verb, eg *hate*
8 an adverb of frequency, eg *often*
9 a noun referring to a quality, eg *faithfulness*
10 a person, eg *bridegroom*

2 (10 marks: 1 mark for each appropriate answer.)

1	OK/all right	6	bored
2	excited	7	patient
3	healthy	8	first
4	embarrassed	9	sad
5	hungry	10	sweet

SECTION 2: GRAMMAR [30 marks]

3a (10 marks: 1 mark for each correct answer.)

1	b) doing	6	a) adore
2	c) going	7	a) where
3	b) used	8	b) do
4	a) for	9	a) to try
5	b) isn't	10	b) don't

b (10 marks: 1 mark for each appropriate answer.)

11	do	16	me
12	when/while	17	every
13	was	18	in/near
14	did	19	but
15	soon	20	mind

4 (10 marks: 1 mark for each correct sentence.)

1 Would you mind opening the door?
2 After he got up, he had breakfast./After getting up, he had breakfast.
3 While I was watching television, she phoned.
4 I wonder if you could repeat that?
5 Before she opened her book, she made a cup of coffee./Before opening her book, she made a cup of coffee.
6 I like to go shopping on Saturday.
7 As we were having lunch, the police arrived.
8 What does this mean?
9 It doesn't matter, does it?
10 She saw him last week.

SECTION 3: READING [20 marks]

5 (2 marks)

a 4
b 2

6 (10 marks: 2 marks for each correct answer.)

a	F	d	F
b	F	e	DS
c	T		

7 (8 marks: 2 marks for each of the four things.)

1 go shopping
2 go to work
3 see the Disneyland fireworks display
4 take a Christmas boat trip

SECTION 4: WRITING [20 marks]

8 (20 marks)

Tell students what you will take into consideration when marking their written work. Criteria should include:
- efficient communication of meaning (7 marks)
- grammatical accuracy (7 marks)
- coherence in the ordering or the information or ideas (3 marks)
- layout, capitalisation and punctuation (3 marks)

It is probably better not to use a rigid marking system with the written part of the test. If, for example, you always deduct a mark for a grammatical mistake, you may find that you are over-penalising students who write a lot or who take risks. Deduct marks if students haven't written the minimum number of sentences stated in the test.

Answers Progress Test 2 Lessons 11–20

SECTION 1: VOCABULARY [30 marks]

1 (10 marks: 1 mark for each correct answer.)

1	force	6	sense
2	clock	7	hall
3	gallery	8	cut
4	tie	9	pen
5	cup	10	minister

2 (10 marks: 1 mark for each word.)

afraid alive apart glad ill ready sorry sure
unable well

3 (10 marks: 1 mark for each appropriate answer.)

1	back	6	up
2	away	7	on
3	in	8	after
4	for	9	down
5	off	10	over

SECTION 2: GRAMMAR [30 marks]

4a (10 marks: 1 mark for each correct answer.)

1	c) haven't written	6	a) can
2	b) ago	7	a) hers
3	c) since	8	b) going to
4	c) supposed	9	c) than
5	c) must	10	c) much

b (10 marks: 1 mark for each appropriate answer.)

11	have	16	for
12	yet	17	more
13	still	18	able
14	certain/sure	19	have/need
15	ever	20	if

5 (10 marks: 1 mark for each correct sentence.)

1 In Perth there are fewer people than in Sydney.
2 Texas is less dangerous/safer than Florida.
3 You're obliged to wear uniform.
4 Should I use the fax?
5 France has more tourists than Germany.
6 Milan is smaller than Rome.
7 I may/might be away.
8 You're not allowed to smoke here.
9 He's certain to write.
10 We still haven't bought a television.

SECTION 3: READING [20 marks]

6 (2 marks)

He was living in Italy.

7 (4 marks: 1 mark for each correct answer.)

1 ✓
2 ✗
3 ✗
4 ✓

8 (6 marks: 1 mark for each correct answer.)

1 F
2 F
3 T
4 T
5 F
6 DS

9 (8 marks: Deduct marks if unimportant information is included.)

The most important points are:
You don't have to pay before you order.
There were comfortable chairs – and they cost no extra.
His coffee was delicious.
He found the English football results.

SECTION 4: WRITING [20 marks]

10 (20 marks)

Tell students what you will take into consideration
when marking their written work. Criteria should
include:
- efficient communication of meaning (7 marks)
- grammatical accuracy (7 marks)
- coherence in the ordering or the information or ideas
  (3 marks)
- layout, capitalisation and punctuation (3 marks)

It is probably better not to use a rigid marking system
with the written part of the test. If, for example, you
always deduct a mark for a grammatical mistake, you
may find that you are over-penalising students who
write a lot or who take risks. Deduct marks if students
haven't written the minimum number of sentences
stated in the test.

Answers Progress Test 3 Lessons 21–30

SECTION 1: VOCABULARY [30 marks]

1a (5 marks: 1 mark for each correct answer.)
1 sitcom   3 peel
2 vulture   4 replaster
                  5 pottery

b (5 marks: 1 mark for each appropriate answer.)
1 a type of film, eg *comedy*
2 an animal (rather than a bird), eg *zebra*
3 a way of cooking, eg *grill*
4 a person who does jobs in the home, eg *plumber*
5 a place where things are made, eg *workshop*

2 (10 marks: 1 mark for each corect answer.)
1 lend   6 buy
2 bring   7 expecting
3 lay   8 watch
4 left   9 lose
5 made   10 checked

3 (10 marks: 1 mark for each correct answer.)
1 lend/give   6 go
2 lose   7 repair
3 clean   8 spread
4 score/get   9 lie
5 catch   10 wait

SECTION 2: GRAMMAR [30 marks]

4a (10 marks: 1 mark for each correct answer.)
1 c) would   6 b) suggested
2 c) make   7 b) him
3 a) as   8 a) is
4 b) excited   9 c) myself
5 c) to be mended 10 b) I'll

b (10 marks: 1 mark for each appropriate answer.)
11 who/that   14 me   17 where
12 if   15 which   18 was
13 told   16 visiting 19 were
                            20 to

5 (10 marks: 1 mark for each correct sentence.)
1 My uncle is an appalling driver.
2 He said he had seen a lion the day before.
3 He asked if soap operas were the most popular programmes.
4 She warned her son to be careful.
5 *The Piano* is the best film (that/which) I have ever seen.
6 She promised she would marry him/me.
7 Football is played all over the world.
8 'I can't find a saucepan,' she said.
9 I'll have the shop assistant wrap up the present.
10 I get on quite well with my parents.

SECTION 3: READING [20 marks]

6 (4 marks)
Australian food is getting better. (1 mark)
Immigrants have brought their own food customs with them. (1 mark)
They have also had a positive effect on Australian food. (1 mark)
There is an amazing range of superb, fresh, locally-produced ingredients. (1 mark)

7 (8 marks: 1 mark for each correct answer.)
1 T   5 DS
2 T   6 T
3 DS   7 F
4 T   8 F

8 (8 marks: Deduct marks if unimportant information is included.)
The most important points are:
The two nations are a) The cities of the southeast and b) remote country areas.
a) In the cities there are a great number of fantastic, international, inexpensive restaurants and cafés featuring almost every imaginable cuisine. Immigration is responsible for this variety.
b) In remote country areas, the eating situation is completely different. Microwavable food and meat pies are the most common items available. The choice is much more limited in country areas.

SECTION 4: WRITING [20 marks]

9 (20 marks)
Tell students what you will take into consideration when marking their written work. Criteria should include:
- efficient communication of meaning (7 marks)
- grammatical accuracy (7 marks)
- coherence in the ordering or the information or ideas (3 marks)
- layout, capitalisation and punctuation (3 marks)

It is probably better not to use a rigid marking system with the written part of the test. If, for example, you always deduct a mark for a grammatical mistake, you may find that you are over-penalising students who write a lot or who take risks. Deduct marks if students haven't written the minimum number of sentences stated in the test.

Answers Progress Test 4 Lessons 31–40

SECTION 1: VOCABULARY [30 marks]

1 (10 marks: 1 mark for each correct answer.)

1	pen	6	lever
2	card	7	phone
3	book	8	oil
4	gum	9	education
5	cube	10	school

2 (10 marks: 1 mark for each correct answer.)

1	bread	6	oil
2	salt	7	cup
3	knife	8	bread
4	apples	9	strawberries
5	fish	10	milk

3 (10 marks: 1 mark for each appropriate answer.)

1	bonnet	6	log
2	fish	7	elevator
3	view	8	sugar
4	bandage	9	head
5	pepper	10	puppy

SECTION 2: GRAMMAR [30 marks]

4a (10 marks: 1 mark for each correct answer.)

1	c) I've fallen	6	c) talks
2	a) did	7	c) wasn't
3	b) saw	8	a) had been sitting
4	c) had finished	9	c) have done
5	b) wouldn't	10	a) had spoken

b (10 marks: 1 mark for each appropriate answer.)

11	and/to	16	doesn't
12	ought	17	case
13	shoudn't	18	could/may might
14	soon	19	have
15	would/might	20	going

5 (10 marks: 1 mark for each appropriate sentence.)

1 I wish I had worked harder.
2 She might have phoned when we were out.
3 I could have left my watch at home.
4 Sally will probably be late.
5 By taking lots of exercise, you can keep fit and healthy.
6 After I had gone out with him for several months, we got married.
7 I might get thirsty so I'll take a drink.
8 If you call a taxi, you won't miss your train.
9 I should have left a tip.
10 I wish I lived in a big house.

SECTION 3: READING [20 marks]

6 (2 marks)

c

7 (2 marks)

Thursday November 7th, 1974

8 (8 marks: 1 mark for each correct answer.)

a	F	e	DS
b	DS	f	F
c	T	g	DS
d	DS	h	F

9 (8 marks: Deduct marks if unimportant information is included.)

The most important points are:
a The name 'Lucky' is linked to the pronunciation of his title – Lucan.
b It is connected with gambling.
c He wasn't really lucky. His marriage had ended in divorce. Perhaps he killed the nanny or was involved in her death. A jury found him guilty of her murder – although he was not present to give his side of the story. Perhaps he himself died. He hasn't seen his children or his friends since the night of the nanny's death.

SECTION 4: WRITING [20 marks]

10 (20 marks)

Tell students what you will take into consideration when marking their written work. Give ten marks for the appropiate layout and forms appropiate for a letter of complaint.
a student's address (2 marks)
b name and address of shop (2 marks)
c greetings, e.g. Dear Sir or Madam (2 marks)
d closing remark, for example, I look forward to hearing from you (2 marks)
e conclusion, for example, Yours faithfully (2 marks)

Give ten marks for the message contained in the letter. Criteria should include:
- efficient communication of meaning (3 marks)
- grammatical accuracy (3 marks)
- coherence in the ordering or the information or ideas (2 marks)
- layout, capitalisation and punctuation (2 marks)

It is probably better not to use a rigid marking system with the written part of the test. If, for example, you always deduct a mark for a grammatical mistake, you may find that you are over-penalising students who write a lot or who take risks. Deduct marks if students have said too much or too little.

Photocopiable